Letters of Love

Letters of Love

Women Political Prisoners
in Exile and the Camps

Compiled and Edited by Julia Voznesenskaya

Translated by Roger and Angela Keys

Quartet Books
London   New York

First published in English by Quartet Books Limited 1989
A member of the Namara Group
27/29 Goodge Street, London W1P 1FD

British Library Cataloguing in Publication Data
Voznesenskaya, Julia, *1941–*
  Letters of love: women political prisoners in
  exile and the camps
  1. Soviet Union. Political prisoners
  I. Title II. Pisma o Lyubvi *English*
  365′.45′0947

ISBN 0–7043–2718–X

Phototypeset by Input Typesetting Ltd, London
Printed and bound in Great Britain by
BPCC Hazell Book Ltd
Member of BPCC Ltd, Aylesbury

Dedicated to my mother,
Olga Nikolayevna Lebedeva,
whose letters gave me comfort
and courage in the camp

Julia Voznesenskaya

Preface to the English Edition

I am glad that my book, *Letters of Love*, which has already been published in West Germany and Holland, is now appearing in English. But what pleases me even more is the fact that it is now an 'historical' book: the writers of all the letters gathered in it are today at liberty.

Gorbachev's 'perestroika' is giving rise to many arguments and contradictory predictions as to its future, from the most optimistic hope that a really dignified way of life may at last be achieved in Russia to sheer terror at the possibility of the cruellest turn of the tide and of new mass repressions. But one thing is not in doubt: of the two hundred political prisoners remaining in places of imprisonment in the USSR today, not one is a woman. This information comes from the bulletin *News from the USSR* edited in Munich by Kronid Lyubarsky, the most reliable publication of its kind.

So is there any cause to be glad that the English reader is now able to read this book, too? I think so, and this is why. When I was in camp myself near Irkutsk, the thing which gave me strength, apart from letters from my relatives, was the knowledge that ordinary people, not politicians at all, from the most diverse countries knew about my fate and supported my family through letters and parcels. *Glasnost* is not simply Gorbachev's present invention, *glasnost* is the thing that his predecessors feared most of all, because behind the closed doors of the State arbitrary power can rule with impunity. The sympathy of friends abroad supported us in the difficult years, and information about what was going on in the camps, prisons and psychiatric hospitals enabled world public opinion to influence events. As a result the prison doors opened wide and hundreds of people were released to freedom. But the camps have not been completely demolished, and building new ones would not take very long under our socialist conditions. So I do not want people in the West to forget about what happened to the heroines of this book only a few years ago. Especially as to this very day not one of them has been formally rehabilitated, not one has had her conviction expunged.

Humanity can overcome the idea and practice of the GULag only by acting together in fellowship – that is what this book is all about.

Julia Voznesenskaya
1 June 1989

From the Editor

I had five days to get ready. What could I manage to do in such a short time? Only one thing: bid farewell to those I loved, say everything possible to them before my journey to the West. As if I could give expression to the whole of the rest of my life.

Luggage? I was leaving with a large bouquet of scarlet tulips (they wanted to confiscate them at the customs, but I refused to give them up) and a plastic bag containing a towel, a box of chocolates (my mother insisted I take them) and a book which I had not had time to finish. Ironically, this was a translation of *The Last Secret* by Nicholas Bethell, a book about the West's handover of Soviet prisoners to Stalin. Banned in the USSR, of course. I had been reading it the day before and wanted to pass it on to one of the friends seeing me off at the airport, but in all the commotion I completely forgot. It couldn't have entered the minds of the customs officers that I was taking out of the country a banned Western book which had been secretly smuggled to me from abroad (later I had to get it back into the USSR; it would have been a pity not to!) Well, I had forgotten to take any toothpaste with me or spare underclothes, either – so before going to sleep I had to wash my one and only set in the sink of my hotel in Vienna and dry them on the radiator. They say that Thomas Mann left Germany with nothing but a travelling bag and an umbrella. So what else should a political exile take with him?

And now year after year has passed, and by various routes my most precious things have gradually begun to make their way back to me, my only riches, abandoned in the country of my birth: my manuscripts, diaries, photographs, letters . . .

Letters from the past. The most precious of them – letters from my friends – from political prisoners, from women friends, letters from the camps and from my various places of exile. Letters of my own, written by me in prison, in camp, in exile. And in addition, there were those letters written to me after I had gone abroad – what routes had they not taken to find me, and how long they took to do so!

And now on the table before me lies my heap of 'treasures'. Letters written on pages torn from school exercise books – there was obviously no other paper available in the humble camp shop; letters written on rough scraps of wrapping paper; letters written on the special forms used by investigators during interrogations; leaves from a diary covered all over with minuscule handwritting. And here is a letter written with indelible pencil on a scrap of prison bedsheet – so there wasn't even a shred of paper left in the cell. A letter written on the back of a page torn from some inane Soviet book about secret-service officers – the letter writer had inflicted damage on the prison library and, as is obvious from the letter, was very proud of it. 'On a page of even the most crass book can be written a couple of wise thoughts,' writes – not very modestly – one female political prisoner from Leningrad.

I decided to compile a book from these letters. Why? Hasn't everything been said about the GULag? There surely cannot be anything that has not been disclosed? In fact, there is a lot. But I do not intend to publish yet another book about how difficult life is for Soviet political prisoners; a great deal has already been written about this, and yet more is bound to be written. Some readers, even some publishers, say: 'That's enough, we're sick of it. We already know EVERYTHING there is to know about it.' But that can't be true, nobody knows EVERYTHING because the people behind the barbed wire not only struggle and suffer, but also love, meditate, share spiritual warmth and mental anxieties with those close to them, speak about love. And in this everyone is completely different from anyone else.

And so I have decided to choose from these letters only those which talk of LOVE: love for children, husbands, lovers, friends, love for poetry and for people, for one's country and for God.

Moreover, I have chosen from the whole pile only letters from women. Why? Not only because after the publication in the West of my *Women's Decameron* I need to justify my title of 'women's writer', and not only because I do actually consider myself to be one. But because . . . How can I express myself more modestly? I shall simply quote to you another Russian writer, Veniamin Kaverin. He once gave an interview on Radio Moscow in which he said that the most difficult thing of all for him was to characterize women: 'Women are generally more complex than men, and their characters deeper.' There you are. And it was not I who said it, but Veniamin Kaverin, a 'men's writer' . . .

When my friends who are also political *émigrés* discovered that I was compiling a book of letters written by women political prisoners, they opened up their own archives and allowed me to make copies of those letters which seemed to be suitable for this book. Some of the letters I came across in collections of *samizdat* material which have found their way through to the West, and some of the letters are my own. Thank you to everybody who helped me.

I shall not dwell on the life stories of the authors of these letters; that is not important. There are many human-rights books published in the West from which you can discover how courageous men and women suffer for their convictions on the islands of the GULag archipelago. There is the 'List of Political Prisoners in the USSR' from which you can discover their names. But I want you to discover their souls, their hearts, their thoughts. And in that case, is it really so very important to know when, and for what unjust sentence, they were placed behind bars? If necessary I shall tell you anything that relates directly to the content of the proffered letters. Just a few words preceding some of them, sometimes an explanatory note. The essence is in the letters themselves.

Oh yes, I forgot to warn you that I am abridging some of the letters. Mainly cutting out paragraphs where greetings are passed on, where the authors ask about their relatives and friends, or where they describe what went on during the investigation or at the court, the reasons why they were imprisoned and how. We have, after all, decided that these are not the most important things. As one female criminal said of political prisoners: 'If they've put them into gaol, it must be for the truth. So long as you've got a person, you can always invent a case.'

When all the letters which I had decided to include in the book had been chosen, they divided themselves up into three bundles: letters to family – husbands, mothers, children; letters to friends, male and female; and love letters. Which group should begin the book? After some thought I decided that it had to begin with letters to friends. There are two reasons for this. In the first place, these letters are more frank in their accounts of camp life and the prisoners' experiences. I can remember myself how in letters to my mother and sons I would painstakingly avoid anything which might upset them, trying always to seem bright and cheerful, making a lot of jokes. I wanted to give them support, to reassure them – and of the worst things that happened to me: say nothing. But to friends you could sometimes complain and even write down the bleak truth; after all, that was why they were friends. My second reason for particularly including letters to friends in the first section is to do with the whole character of the planned book. This book is not for politicians, nor for historians, nor for Sovietologists. This book has been put together for those readers who are able to read the letters of the women prisoners as though they were the recipients: as friends.

When you come to the letters in the second section,

written to children, husbands, mothers and relatives, you will already know a great deal about camp life and you will be able to tell for yourselves when the authors are hiding the truth – so as not to distress their nearest and dearest – and where a joke and cheerful words conceal their love and their anguish.

Now about the third section: letters to a lover. It is not unusual for the authorities to use repressive measures, simultaneously or one by one, against husband and wife, an engaged couple, or against people who are simply in love. Often this is done deliberately and with exquisite cruelty. This is what happened to Tanya Osipova and her husband Vanya Kovalyov, for example. In May 1980 they arrested Tanya and then sentenced her to five years' imprisonment in camp, to be followed by five years' internal exile, but Vanya Kovalyov they arrested only in August 1981, sentencing him later for the same number of years and under the same Article 70 of the Russian Federation Criminal Code ('anti-Soviet propaganda') for belonging to the same Moscow–Helsinki Group. For a long time after this both Tanya and Vanya themselves, as well as friends imprisoned in the camps and free at home and abroad, fought so that they might be given the right to see each other. This right was granted.

But for those who were not man and wife, who were simply in love with one another and who had been placed in different camps, there was no hope. Even sending letters from one camp to another was forbidden, let alone meetings. And yet people continued to love one another and write letters to each other – with the help of friends, through channels unknown to the authorities. And now one such secret correspondence between imprisoned lovers has fallen into my hands. True to the principle underlying this book, I include only the woman's letters.

Of the dozens of letters from women prisoners one seemed to me to deserve special attention, a letter telling not simply of the camps themselves, but also of the place which the camps occupy in the actual structure of Soviet society. And, above all else, this is a letter of love. I thought that it might serve as a key to the whole book.

You now see that book before you.

Julia Voznesenskaya

First Bundle

Letters to Friends,
Male and Female

From camp – to a woman friend

... You know yourself that this world is far from being the only thing that we have to look forward to. It is only the 'training ground' after all – an experimental zone where the process of transforming man with a small 'm' into Man with a capital goes on (let us use a capital letter to emphasize the difference for the time being, even though another word or concept may crop up later on). Man has only one possible direction, only one course of study: the subject of Love. We are only just beginning to suspect this. Me, too. Camp is a good classroom for this curriculum.

Fantasy writers who lack imagination can only attribute the discovery and development of new modes of communication to the science of the future. And scientists have been concerned to label this, too: as parapsychology. But Love has known all about it for years and years.

Love has revealed to us the ability to read thoughts at a distance, communication by means of the slightest, scarcely perceptible signals, foreknowledge, the possibility of influencing the behaviour of another person through thought, and finally – the resurrection of the dead. When Love becomes perfect, so will we. Perfect, happy and all-powerful. (And I know you realize this, too.)

But the question arises: if this has long been familiar to some people, then why has it not become clear to everybody?

You know, I have met people in the camp who are afraid of freedom – of the responsibility which it confers, of the need to take decisions. A concentration camp is a masterpiece in its own way: humanity has elevated its basest instincts into a symbol and constructed a model of this. A concentration camp is a symbol of the anti-future, the ideal incarnation of 'humanity's dream, born of labour and battle' (Vladimir Mayakovsky). Just give people a little bit more to eat – and there are your 'glass palaces' for you, total contentment and freedom from anxiety, existence totally simplified and complete, according to the Communist interpretation.

And with the complete absence of Love. Relationships are reduced to the simple-minded satisfaction of basic needs, completely pure and innocent, as with animals. Procreation is stimulated by the authorities: additional rations, reduced working day and subsequently – possible amnesty for the successful mother.

Children here are not in fact brought up by their mothers or by common-or-garden nannies, but by women prisoners specially assigned to them. At least initially they are still kept with their mothers – the problem of artificial feeding has not yet been solved.

Males from the neighbouring men's camp are brought here in formation, ostensibly to work. In fact, 'duty visits to the women's compound' are a reward for those who are 'firmly embarked upon the path of reform' and for simple informers. The actual selection of candidates has also to do with their external male characteristics, of course. 'What's this you've brought us?' the women hurl at the team leader, if the new arrival doesn't appeal to anyone (which happens extremely rarely, let it be added).

Homosexuality flourishes in the camp as well. Although, to give the women their due, it isn't as humiliating in character as in the men's compound where the passive partners are subjected to all kinds of indignity and, in general, are reduced to a sub-human level. In the women's compound an active lesbian is the *kobyol* or butch female, and her partner simply a woman like anyone else. Isn't this evidence of the age-old inequality of the sexes? A woman playing the part of a man is a person of the highest order, while a man playing the part of a woman is the lowest form of life.

The majority of our women are 'auto-sterilized', however

– by the methods of cold, hunger, endless depression, illness, physical exhaustion and chronic lack of sleep. Half the women have stopped menstruating. People say that it starts again after you have left the camp, but who has checked up on that? And the thing as a whole is frightening because you can become accustomed to it.

And what unity of opinion there exists here, what order, what stable fulfilment and overfulfilment of plans, what universal political involvement! Once a week after work they herd everyone together again to make us listen to the testament of happiness in living and working under the leadership of our dear Party and Government.

I have been lucky, my dear: I am already living under Communism today. But what gives me consolation, what inspires me with hope is the fact that the whole of humanity will not be driven into camps; and even here sparks flicker up time and again – sparks of love, humanity, kindness, heroism for the sake of one's neighbour. And how people yearn for their children here, their loved ones!

After all Love does not go away, does not vanish, and is not cut off because of separation. As one of our women poets has written: 'In separation constancy is simple / And flame-proof stand its bridges.' Love never leaves – it is ourselves who sometimes abandon it. But if it has existed at all, then it still – *is*. Somewhere in this world, in the very essence of our soul. Relationships may finish, but Love always remains stamped into our soul, our character, our eyes.

This is why I keep on saying to you over and over again that one doesn't need to learn anything except Love. Other knowledge will come later, and a great deal – that which is most important – will be revealed through Love itself.

And that is how your love warms me from afar (once again this winter they have brought hardly any coal at all into our compound!)

From exile, where the author was transferred from camp – to a man friend

My dear friend,

At last I am able to write to you, after so many years . . .
You have asked me many questions about what has happened and about what is happening now. It is easier to
answer the latter, so it is with these answers I shall begin.
What is Beyneu, the place where I am exiled? The most
important thing is that this is already my third place of
exile, the third district. All three are in the Mangyshlak
region. The first place was Shetpe, the centre of Mangistau
district. I was there from 3 November to 9 February 1984.
I was working as a hospital orderly in a polyclinic and
living in a separate (!) one-room flat with running water,
a toilet and central heating. I had only just begun to
get things together, acquired some furniture, hung up the
curtains, when they transferred me to Tauchik. The way
they did it was extremely barbaric: they simply took me
by force, without any warning, without giving a reason or
showing me any authorization, and with a convoy of militia
they took me to the next place of exile. Suffice it to say
that my dismissal from the polyclinic was effected by an
order dated 3 February, that is to say a week earlier, about
which I had known nothing; the order itself they concealed
from me, but the wording, as I managed to find out a lot
later, was not according to an article of the Labour Code,
but 'on the instructions of the militia'(!) My belongings
were brought to me a couple of days later by my sister,
who had been staying with me at the time. Tauchik is a
small settlement (a State camel stockfarm), with a popu-
lation one hundred per cent Kazakh, many of them not
understanding any Russian at all. It isn't the district

centre; that's about 100 km. away at Mangyshlak (near Shevchenko, the chief town of the region). The district is very long and zigzaggy, like a snake, and so the road which the bus runs along from Tauchik to the district centre crisscrosses other districts several times. And as you know, an exile is only allowed to move freely within the one district. So it turned out that I wasn't allowed to travel to the district centre, or so I was informed by the militia. I began demanding a transfer to the district centre. This went on for about six months as they decided one thing and then changed their minds, saying that they were transferring us to the village of Mangyshlak and that they were 'looking for a flat' for me there, and then finally moving me to Beyneu, the centre of the Beyneu district. Compared with the first two places, this is the foulest of all. As flat as a table-top, not a single tiny hill, empty steppe all around, an extremely melancholy landscape. As far as everything else is concerned, the accommodation and work are also much worse. But then on the other hand, it is a district centre, that's to say it has a polyclinic, library, telephone office where you can make trunk calls, and so on. The food supply here is fairly good: you can get vegetables, potatoes, dried milk, cottage cheese, liver, even pure butter. None of this is available very often, but I have a refrigerator. The shop in Tauchik had only millet, sugar, sunflower oil and bread every other day. My work is tedious to the nth degree; imagine life as an accounts clerk working out wages, compiling various credit and debit documents, etc. I have to sit at a desk from nine till six with an hour for lunch, even when there is no work to do. I receive eighty roubles per month with a 30% supplement for living in the back of beyond, that is to say 104 roubles altogether. In other organizations the supplement is 60% or 70%, but on what basis I don't really understand. There are a large number of Russians, and many of them, probably the majority, have come here for the extra salary. There are a lot of two-storeyed houses here with all mod cons. The area where I live is called Desolation – wooden shanties without any conveniences, very old, left over from earlier times when the settlement was only beginning to be built. They get their water from wells here, and they don't know how to winch it up, either. They simply lower their buckets down on a piece of rope, each person using his own. As for toilets – well, as everywhere in Mangyshlak, that's a question of going wherever you need to go and taking a shovel with you. It has turned cold now, and the flies have disappeared. In October there were still clouds of them. My room is ten metres square and there's a kitchen, but the entrance is shared with neighbours. The stove is wrecked, the doors don't shut tightly, and you're not allowed to cut in a keyhole, so I've got a padlock dangling down, like on a barn door. There's no ventilation window at all. When they first brought me to Beyneu, I began by living in the hotel. Then they offered me this flat and a job, saying that there was no other flat available and that this one belonged to the comptometer centre where I would have to go and work. This was work that I really did *not* want, but there was no way out. They began to put pressure on me to leave the hotel while at the same time promising everything: we'll repair the flat, retrieve your belongings, fix you a place at the kindergarten (my four-year-old granddaughter has been living with me since 7th September).

At the end of September somebody rang me up at midnight and demanded that I leave the hotel within twenty-four hours. When I asked whom I was speaking to, the voice replied: 'That doesn't matter. We are people who are interested that you get out as quickly as possible.' I wrote a complaint to the chief of the militia about this threatening behaviour, and his reply was: 'It'll be sorted out.' And perhaps it was. At the present moment things are like this. Lena goes to the kindergarten (the children are *all* Kazakhs, the teachers are Russian and Kazakh). They started repairing the flat and then gave up: 'Do it yourself!'

The stove is still standing there useless, without a hotplate and other metal parts. They said: 'We won't repair it – you don't get stoves like that now. These are old houses and we don't put people in them any more.' They did bring me my belongings – at the end of October, but up till then Lena and I had had to live off the floor. And the business of getting my things was absolutely absurd. I had sent them off in a container train, which was supposed to arrive on 10 September. It transpired that there is no container station here. Goods arrive at Kulsary, and you have to bring them the 250 km. from there to here by car. Then it turned out that the container hadn't been unloaded at Kulsary and for some reason had gone on to Kzyl-Orda, and when it would make the return journey nobody knew. In the middle of October I arrived at Kulsary, but there was no car to be hired, and anyway if you did manage to find one it would cost you 260 roubles. During all this various 'well-wishers' offered three times either to give me a car or even to transport my things for me, but on each occasion it turned out that what they had in mind was payment 'for services rendered'. In the end the militia helped me out, to the tune of seventy roubles.

All these changes of place and work have deprived me of any holiday and any chance of visiting my relatives. Next year I want to visit Pskov region to see all my grandchildren who will be staying there in a dacha. If they let me go . . . Of my eight grandchildren I have met only five so far. I miss Tauchik. At least there was some countryside there: hills, ravines, a variety of bird-life; I even saw some *dzeren* once, not to mention hares, tortoises, ground squirrels, and so on. But they wouldn't let me have my granddaughter there – there was nothing to eat, there were no doctors, there was no telephone. And besides, I was given no choice in the situation: an exile has the right to travel to the district centre and to choose a place to live within the district; but 'they' have the right to choose a 'suitable' district, choose an 'appropriate' flat and are able to compel you to take up 'the right employment'.

I don't measure time by years now, but by summers: one summer out of five has already passed. Summertime here is murderous – 45° in the shade. Lena will be living with me until June.

. . . You were asking me what SHIZO and PKT are.* I have a little experience in this respect – eight days of SHIZO and two months' PKT. I shall try to describe them. Prisoners are placed in SHIZO for periods up to fifteen days. It is a small cell with two sets of double bunks, rather like a railway sleeper, except that during the day all four of them are raised and locked into position. In the middle is a child's table, very low, and also four low blocks of wood for sitting on, or two benches. In the corner stands the latrine bucket, very heavy and fastened to the wall with a chain. There's nothing else. The window is covered with a closely-latticed grille, and has many panes of glass missing so that, although it has double glazing, there is a terrible draught. The floor is made of wood, but beneath the boards is a layer of concrete, forty or fifty centimetres thick. You're not allowed to have anything with you in the cell – paper, pen, books, toilet requisites – none of these is allowed. You get special clothing for SHIZO, very thin. You're not allowed anything made of wool. The food is very sparse, given every other day, and on the 'empty' day you get nothing but three lots of bread and boiling water. For me the most excruciating thing was the cold, and the second, having nothing at all to do. Theoretically, you can be given SHIZO with provision for work outside, which is easier, but women politicals aren't given work as that would entail contact with the female work assigner who is a common criminal. The temperature in September–October 1983 when I was there used to dip as low as 13° in the PKT cells and possibly even lower. I managed to get them

---

* Two types of isolation unit (translators' note).

to measure the temperature on three occasions – and every time it was 13° (by law it should never be less than 16°). When I was in PKT I saw (or rather, heard) a lot of women from the criminal camp, locked up in SHIZO or PKT (the cells are identical; it's only the conditions in which you're held that differ). Some of them used to get several periods of SHIZO consecutively, up to forty-five days.

I came to realize that SHIZO is the vilest thing, crippling people both physically and morally. And it doesn't matter what offences people get it for. I saw (or again heard, as you can hear everything through the walls) that they don't sleep on their bunks, but on the floor – it turns out to be warmer that way if there are four or five people in the cell: you can sleep if you give each other warmth. Many women get ovary or kidney infections. In PKT things are easier: they give you a mattress, a thin blanket, bedclothes, warmer clothing, half an hour's exercise. And above all – you are able to read. The food is just as meagre, but you do get it every day. You're allowed to smoke. You are allowed to spend two roubles at the camp shop (as long as you aren't deprived of this at the time you are sentenced to a stretch of PKT). If only those who have legalized these things were made to spend even as little as twenty-four hours in SHIZO themselves.

I know that after I left the compound my friends had a lot of SHIZO and PKT. I know that they will never accept this situation, that they will protest – by refusing to work and by means of hunger-strikes. And that because of these protests they will get new sentences of SHIZO and PKT or even a new term of imprisonment in camp. I think about them constantly – about Irina Ratushinskaya, Tanya Osipova, Natasha Lazareva, Galya Barats, Yadviga Belyauskene, Raya Rudenko. How will they last out till the end of their terms? Will they survive? . . . The main rule of the camps is that you must not intercede on behalf of others. They will never reconcile themselves to this rule.

From camp – to friends

May peace dwell in your hearts!

It is already nearly two years since walls separated us and now there is distance, too. But I do not lose heart, and I even rejoice because 'blessed are they who are exiled for the truth'.

It is two years since the duty warder rattled his keys behind me, and I found myself alone in a cell with barred windows. I was not afraid of anything, but I burst into tears. And the words of a prayer came into being by themselves: 'Father, I wish these bonds to become a test of my faithfulness to Thee, but not to be a temptation.' And now I always feel Him close by me. I sleep, and He protects me. Always and in everything, even amid those who perish around me. He gives me joy and courage. People ask me: 'How can you be happy? Do you not long to go home?' And the deputy governor said to me: 'But it's a crime – your being here. You could do so much good if you were free!' To which I replied that God can see where I do the most good. I am needed here, too, by those who are despised by everyone.

But when I am alone, I think: but I am a person just like them, why then are they unable, totally unable to rejoice? They are forever angry and impatient. And immediately the answer comes: their father is the father of lies, deceit, evil, of all that degrades and defiles a human being, and they bow down low to him. Whereas our Father is the Father of truth and light who has given us eternal life and who said: 'Rejoice and be glad, for great is your reward in heaven.' How then can we lose heart? That is why joy is forever both in my heart and on my face.

It is so difficult, though, to tear oneself away from this constant stir, to overcome fear and timidity and dedicate oneself entirely to Christ, bringing the light to others in both intense heat and freezing cold. You must be resolute, too, my dear friends. Fill the places as they become empty so that His cause should not lack workers. For when old age and debility come upon us, we shall no longer be able to take the work upon ourselves, having strength only to attend services.

In my correspondence with friends I rejoice at the sight of their bright and lively spirits. I shall answer their letters, and they with just such joy will raise my spirit again in their replies. I write regularly to one sister in the faith who writes back little, and on postcards, but whose words I read with such delight as if I were present at a discussion among friends.

Friends, I am grateful to you for everything. I thank you for your prayers, through which I live and from which I gain courage.

May the God of peace and love dwell with you always. I wish you strength.

From camp – to friends

My dear friends,

I want to explain my motives for beginning a hunger-strike, if Vanka and I are not given the opportunity to see each other. I want to explain because all my friends will be worried and will perhaps try to dissuade me.

The KGB's tactics with regard to Vanka and myself were clear from the first moment of my arrest: they promised that we would go together. I got into the car and he was pushed away. After that either the judge would neglect to see him, or the letter in which the administration of the Lefortovo prison gave permission for a meeting would arrive just after I had already been sent elsewhere, or the visitors' block would happen to be under repair, or a quarantine order would be imposed. Before each visit the KGB men would try to talk to me and each time I would refuse to speak to them – the result is obvious. And both times they didn't simply prevent the whole visit, they forced Vanka actually to come along: let him get ready first, travel, hope, wait – so that it affects us even worse. After Vanka himself was arrested, they admitted to me openly that they could have permitted a meeting in Compound 5, but that they 'did not consider it expedient'. And now, even though I applied to them with a request that he should be sent here, they have despatched him to Perm, because according to 'regulations', meetings between convicted persons 'held in different corrective labour institutions are not permitted'.

During the course of the investigation they tried to condition me to the idea that Vanka would betray me, that he was already doing so, that he would forget me, abandon me – but they didn't succeed. If they don't manage to destroy our love for each other, it means that they will have to use our love itself to break us, just as my longing to have children was for them a way of compelling me to take part in the investigation,* and if they don't succeed in breaking us through that means, then they let us suffer even more miserably so that we won't want to go back to camp again. And can I, after all this, humbly and meekly just accept the impossibility of seeing Vanka? An impossibility which consists merely of a bloody-minded manoeuvre on the KGB's part: 'We don't want to and we won't let you.' No, of course not. Not on your life!

And there's a second reason. Apart from their tactics in relation to Vanka and myself, there is a general directive not to permit meetings between relations who are in prison, a special secret instruction about not holding relatives in

---

* The author of the letter was pregnant at the time of her arrest. While in prison she had a miscarriage and she needed the assistance of a doctor, who could be summoned only on the authority of an investigator.

22

the same camp. When Raya asked whether she and her husband would have had the right to meet if he had not been transferred, they answered her bluntly: 'Yes, you would, and that is why we had him transferred.' And there was Galina Silivonchik who actually found herself in the same camp as her brother (either it was before the directive was issued, or somebody had slipped up). Her brother is just like a son to her; she raised him from the cradle. After her husband had been killed trying to steal a plane, her whole life was entirely concentrated on her brother. Almost ten years they spent in the same camp with only a road separating them, but they were never ever allowed to see each other.

In the literature produced for the camp administration it is explained that meetings between prisoners help maintain socially useful relations. But then families like ours, Galina, the KGB does *not* need. They are social relations which it is necessary not to maintain, but to destroy. And now that whole families have begun to be imprisoned, it is essential to resist this vile policy.

If I do manage to secure a meeting, it will be important to many more than just myself and Vanka. And if I should die, on the other hand, then that will not be in vain, either: the struggle will be carried on after me, and the KGB are hardly likely to risk another fatal outcome.

So there: you see that my hunger-strike is not just a sudden whim, not an act of desperation, but a calm and carefully considered determination to fight.

I should like to cope with this by myself, without Vanka, but if you consider it necessary, then let him know. And if he then wants to support me, may God be on the side of both of us.

With fond kisses.

In transit – to a friend in exile

Greetings to my poor, abandoned Vorkutan convict.

I am already up to my ears in trees. From Seida station onwards birch trees have been passing by the window – the same size as me, so you can imagine what 'giants' they are. And in Kotlas itself, where I am kicking my heels, there are proper wooden houses. With carved window-frames. The windows in the prison cell are also 'carved' – through the hole which someone has cut into the metal strips you can see the tops of two poplars.

Imagine, Zhenechka, the people breathe air! After Vorkuta with its lack of oxygen, I am intoxicated. The air isn't for everyone, of course, and isn't continual – our exercise period lasts only an hour. But on the other hand, during these periods I live for the whole hour and I don't feel as if I'm on my last legs.

Zhenya, a strange and terrible thing happened to me on the journey, and you will not be pleased with me: I have removed my cross and given it to a murderer. This man saved me from being attacked by drunken guards in the railway carriage. This is how it happened. Perhaps I could have got out of the situation myself, but he intervened and threatened to kill them. 'You know that I've got nothing to lose, boys, don't you? I've already notched up two dead cops . . . ' Later I found out that he was being taken to court where the death sentence was definitely waiting for him. It's actually a long story, so I'll tell you all the details another time. The gist is, he saw the cross around my neck and said to me: 'I have never believed in God, but I suddenly sense that things will be easier for me if I have the cross.' And so I gave it to him. He immediately became so calm and cheerful and spent the rest of the journey singing idiotic prison songs to me and trying to persuade me 'not to look so glum'. And this was *him* telling *me*! I don't grudge him the cross, but I feel a bit scared myself without it. I have already got used to it protecting me everywhere from everything bad. It was given to me by my mother. So that's my story, Zhenya. And now can you, as a seasoned prisoner, give me advice on how to get hold of another cross? Can you get official permission for one? I could ask somebody to bring me one, but I don't want any visits. I instinctively feel that I'll spend a long time yet being dragged around the country, and then they'll take me to Baikal or to Sakhalin or somewhere. Vorkuta usually sends its criminal ladies to Kungur or Surgut, but then I am not a Vorkuta lady. I'm much more dangerous than that. My people know how to get through to me even across the Urals. Do you remember the trouble my friend caused the Vorkuta KGB? Now they'll try to hide me away as far as possible from my friends. And travelling to visit me will be long and expensive. That's why I think that from now on I shall have to sacrifice any visits. It would be too much of a luxury, Zhenya, don't you think?

In the transit camps I draw and write poetry, and on the trains I spend most of my time talking to people.

It's terribly hot and stuffy in the cell – we've got people on the floor and under the bunks. I must make my way over to the window and swallow a bit of air, so I'll finish the letter now.

Well, farewell and don't grieve for me.

Many kisses . . .

Letter to a friend sentenced for the same crime and now released from camp

Greetings

I received your telegram, both letters and even the 'Crucifixion'.* Thank you, my friend, for thinking about me straight away.

Things are all right – I am alive. That is the main and most astonishing thing. You know very well all the specific conditions under which I live, but it is still MY LIFE, that is to say: I don't feel as though I'm Eurydice in Hades. I am being released on 26 June next year. I hope to survive till that date, but nobody has given me any guarantees – that's specific conditions for you, brother!

My dear friend, I'm not writing about how glad I am that you have returned to Peter;** that is obvious. But I am even more glad about your relative well-being during those first days back, your joy and good spirits. It is a pity that you mention nothing of your first hours of freedom, of being reunited with friends and how it went off. You might have shared your experiences! I think about this with some uncertainty – how will it be for me, how do things go in general?

. . .

You know, how difficult life is for a normal person here. There is nobody here who is capable of putting together two sentences in a row without making a mistake or swearing. Ignorance is a very boring thing. The countryside around the camp is amazingly beautiful, it is true. For two weeks we were taken outside the compound to plant potatoes – with sub-machine-guns pointing at us and accompanied by alsatians. It's about five kilometres to the field, plenty of time to feast my eyes on my surroundings!

It's a strange life and a strange world. All waiting to be put on the screen. I look and listen, chatting a lot to people, writing the odd thing down.

. . .

Write to me about your plans, my friend, about the

Photograph of an icon.
*** A still common colloquial term for the city of Petersburg – Leningrad (translators' note).*

changes which you found in Peter. Pray for me so that I can get out of this morass as quickly as possible – how loathsome it has all become! Just to glimpse one familiar human face out of the corner of my eye would be a joy. The things I witness every day you wouldn't even see in a zoo. And you feel sorry for them all to the point of anguish, to the point where you would be willing to sacrifice your own life if only a stop could be made to the working of this infernal machine for the transformation of weak people into even weaker slaves.

Goodbye – and success to you in your new life!

From camp – to a woman friend

This is the dream I dreamed.
On a white field horses stood.
The gentle sway of their bodies swayed the field itself.
And the whole of nature was swaying in rhythm.
The same rhythm caught by a captive balloon.
And by seaweed in watery freedom.

Marvellous, isn't it?

Do you know who wrote it? Otar Chiladze, my friend here. Only he doesn't know anything about it at all – because he's living quite happily somewhere in Georgia – and will he ever know that, once upon a time (and the very first time during my imprisonment), a mobile book-shop came to the camp? In the middle of all kinds of unreadable Soviet junk I suddenly caught sight of a small book of verse, opened it at random – and now I have a friend, Otar Chiladze!

A kind of wisdom, perhaps – passionate and radiant? That's how I have defined his verse. I know nothing about him and I can't guess from his poetry which compartment of hell has been his particular fate, but I can feel that he is acquainted with the place. He is not only a wise man, but a warrior, and that has become a rare quality in poetry (not so rare in Georgian poetry, perhaps, but then Otar writes in Russian). Can you remember my saying more than once that poetry is now awaiting and craving heroes, not these lyric or civic poets. I implore you to look out for his poetry.

Things are all right for me. And for Yura. There was a hope that it would get easier for him, but . . . He and I face yet another terrible winter apart. He has been my salvation until now, supporting me with all his heart. Now, I fear, he will have less strength, so it is my turn. But perhaps it just seems to me at this moment that he is worse off and that I am stronger. He will probably carry on 'supporting me in his arms' even at such a distance! He is very strong, my Yura. And believe it or not, we do seem to be happy, the two of us, in spite of everything, even separation. His heart may be so far away, but it is my heart, too, and it beats for me. And a heart like this is essential, somewhere to retreat, if only for a moment, to shelter from the relentless hardship. Perhaps this is a weakness, this insane craving to be needed by someone, to be for somebody not just a memory, but living, today, existing and needed *today*.

But if this is weakness, then what is love for? For fair weather, to enhance a prosperous life, mutual pleasure? That's all very well and good, but it can be snatched away so easily! On the other hand, the love that Yura and I have – let them just try and steal *that* away . . .

How are you feeling now? Is it going to be soon? You say that people have given you too many baby vests? Why don't you sew little mittens out of the ones you don't need and put them on those little fingers during the first month so that its hands are free and it doesn't scratch its nose? And one more piece of advice from an experienced old mother: be sure you make a few romper-suits for the very first month – a child should have freedom of movement!

In the shops they only sell romper-suits for children of four months and over, and until that age babies are supposed to be swaddled, as though they were in a prison. By the way, your baby's freedom is your freedom: the more a small child is free to move, tossing and turning around as it likes, the more soundly it will sleep later on. And that will be your time of freedom.

My dear, you must get hold of two important books from somewhere: *Our Child* by Mirka Fignerová (a translation from the Czech) and *Baby and Child Care* by Benjamin Spock. Fignerová writes about children up to the age of one, and Spock about the whole of childhood. They're the best books that I ever got to see. If you can't buy them or borrow them from friends, don't do nothing. Spend a few days in the library and copy them out – it's worth the bother!

Many kisses.

From camp – to a woman friend

Dear Tanechka,

I want to write to you first about the visit. I have been so happy these last three days. The children have put my mind at rest completely, have removed my greatest worry: anxiety about them. It now seems that I shall sit out the rest of my sentence in peace. What beautiful children I have, don't you think? Aren't I a very lucky person? I'll carry on here, and at home everything will be all right.

I sometimes forget to thank the Lord in my prayers in even the simplest words for this love: the love of my children and relations, and of my friends. But I begin every day with a feeling of thankfulness towards Him. Not for the fact that I am still alive, but because life carries on in its fullness, and no one takes anything away from it. As for the cold, hunger, the filth and vulgarity – that's no longer important.

I have acquired an adoptive daughter here, a Tatar girl called Zukhra, eighteen years old. It happened like this. A new intake of prisoners arrived one day, among them a dirty and embittered girl. Like lightning word flew round the whole compound that she's got syphilis. There are a couple of dozen such beauties here. Their illness is no longer at the dangerous stage for the people around them: it's already been cured, or so the doctors tell us. But you can quite well understand people's attitude to these 'syphilitics' – they're squeamish about them, wary. And that makes the sufferers angry and bitter, of course. To begin with my Zukhra just couldn't ignore any of the scenes and fights which often take place in the camp. She would be right in the middle of every brawl, down and feathers flying everywhere. One fine day she turned up at the building-site with us. Then our team happened to pick on one little chit and began to torment her. I stood up for her when the whole gang wanted to beat her up: 'Can't you sort it out by talking about it? Why are you all ganging up on one person, like a pack of rats?' The women then began to explain the crime she was supposed to have committed. Certainly, the girl was at fault: she had stolen something from someone else's parcel. All the same I managed to persuade them to leave beating her up, and simply send her to Coventry. Then Zukhra rushed up to me, saying: 'And why is this one sticking up for a thief? Perhaps she's a thief herself?' Our women laughed at such a suggestion, and I smiled at her and said in deliberate teacher's tones: 'And you, little girl, should learn to keep your nose out of grown-up business. And that tongue of yours needs to be kept in check, too. I've been meaning to tell you for quite a while that it's appalling for a young girl like you to use such foul language.' I must tell you that most of what Zukhra comes out with is untranslatable and unquotable for censorship reasons – real gutter filth. She burst out laughing at my remark and said in an insolent voice: 'Some little girl you've found! I stopped being a girl at twelve years old, if you must know! Do you know what I was sentenced for?'

'Yes, I know,' I replied calmly, 'and I've seen enough ruined and unhappy girls like you before. When I was moving around from camp to camp, there were any number of under-age girls who had been doing your sort of work. But whatever your life may have been like out there, to me you are still just a little girl – the same age as my sons. And I would ask you, at least when you're with me, to behave as a young girl of your age ought to behave.'

She was amazed, clapped her mouth shut and walked off. But at lunchtime, after I had hurriedly spooned down my revolting bowl of soup in the canteen and grabbed my bread ration and departed with my notebook to a secluded spot on the site, Zukhra came sidling up to me and asked: 'What's that you're writing?' (Notice that she was already using the polite form of address.)

'I'm writing poetry,' I replied. 'Would you like to hear it?'

Well, during the half-hour that remained of lunchtime I tamed her for ever. Two weeks later my pupil signed on at school, and she and I have begun on our intensive programme of work. I have come to an agreement with the teachers that they will let her take her secondary exams as an external pupil – at home she abandoned school at fifteen. Now your poor old friend is having to relearn mathematics, which I grew to hate at school myself. The girl has given herself a good wash, combed her hair nicely and . . . blushes whenever she hears a swear word. True, she looks around at me when this happens and turns red as if the swearing offends my ears rather than hers, but for educational purposes it doesn't make any difference.

I am struck by one thing: it was so easy for me to take her in hand, she so quickly and wholeheartedly responded not just to kindness, but rather to the fact of being treated as a young girl. Isn't this whole monstrously huge Soviet educational machine of ours capable of making even one simple, natural movement in the direction of an unhappy child like this? How many of these poor souls have I met in the transit camps, how often have I recited stories to them, combed lice from their hair, listened to their own pathetic and frightening tales! And always they would cling to me, like mushrooms to an old tree-stump, huddling up to me, yearning for the kind, stern words of their mothers. I feel infinitely sorry for them because nobody is concerned about their education or re-education and the camps just nurture them into one thing: hardened, dyed-in-the-wool criminals from childhood onwards, to the grief of others and of themselves.

So that is the child I have found for myself here. Well, give my own little one a kiss from me.

From camp – to a woman friend

Greetings, darling!

> Gonna get myself a stagecoach,
> Rattle on thro' bullets and dust.
> I'm a last-chance desperado,
> Cheat that ol' baddie fate I must.
> Song from a Western

Now, do you feel like dying with absolute envy, you sophisticated Petersburg lady? Well, then, picture for yourself our valley, called Death Valley by the prisoners. It is cordoned off on all sides from the rest of the world by hills. The local inhabitants call them 'slopes', but after reading the verse of Brodsky and Aronzon the word 'hills' sounds much more poetic. These hills obviously conceal within themselves not only the bones of prisoners 'released before their time' (as we call those who die here and never taste freedom again), but also the secret graves of drifters killed in the taiga, fragments of clay idols, animal lairs and gold. Whereas 'slope' just conveys stone, sand, bushes, pines, nothing romantic at all. Slopes are good only for wild rosemary in bud. In the valley stands our reservation. And now along the track between the dilapidated wigwams (wooden huts) a cowboy lopes along on a chestnut mustang. The cowboy is, of course, me, and the mustang – an old gelding called Lord. The two of us are cheerful, slightly shabby, stumbling a bit, and the fresh air makes our heads spin, but all the same we feel exactly like cowboy and mustang. We are carrying cement to the building-site (the loading of the cement I shall leave out of the scene, as a spectacle unsuitable for those of a nervous disposition, and anyway you can't actually see anything as the cloud of cement completely swathes us from the end of my nose to the top of my stallion's tail). I talk to Lord exclusively in English. And so as not to put me in an embarrassing position, Lord pretends that he understands English as well as he does the obscene language of the other women. He obeys without question. Seated on this 'death-bed' saddle, I feel as if I am on Pegasus on Parnassus and in Texas all at the same time. Sometimes instead of Lord I am brought a filly a lot younger and friskier called Zoryana. Zoryana and I also get on well with each other, but Lord remains my first big equine love. Well, what do you think, are you already bursting with envy?

Who would have imagined me having to follow such a strange route finally to realize the crystal dream of my childhood: to hold in my hand the reins of a real, live horse! Here's to my KGB investigator!

The other aspects of life here are not bad, either. Obviously, lack of poetic talent is now beginning to show itself: after all, normal geniuses die aged thirty-seven to the man.*

---

* Alexander Pushkin died aged thirty-seven (translator's note).

I am presently thirty-seven, conditions for dying are the best imaginable, but I am making arrangements to do so!

And you, my dear, when will you learn to put blank envelopes in your letters? Poverty in camp in terms of absoluteness can be compared only with that of kings, and I have in mind King Lear. In a word, if you want letters from me, let me have envelopes for them! And tell our mutual friends one more thing, that I can't remember all their addresses from memory, so it's best for everyone to write it on the envelopes. It's not so very dangerous.

Do write to me. The terrible, long winter is already on the wane, but letters are necessary all the same: they make you feel calmer, you begin to believe that the world surrounding you is far from being the only thing in store for you. Write about everything in detail, both about those who are in the same position as I am, and about those who have travelled even further away. And what has happened to Zhenya P.? Why is he silent? I know that this means things must be difficult for him and he doesn't want to trouble me with despondent letters. But don't forget about him, I implore you. I do at least have a bit of sun, while he has the arctic night. Brrr . . .

Kisses to you all. I love you and see you all in my happier dreams.

From camp – to a woman friend

My dear friend,

It was only today that I got to see the newspapers dated 15 July 1978.* I didn't even come across them myself, but camp-buddies brought them along and asked for an explanation. Well, things are certainly happening in the

---

* Reports concerning the trial of Orlov and Shcharansky.

damned West, that much-vaunted Europe!* I knew almost nothing except for an allusion by Gusar in a letter – and how much could he write, anyway? Just a hint or two . . .

And all this time I have been busy with my offspring, my camp pupil, Zukhra. The offspring hasn't turned out at all badly, being both affectionate and loyal. Well, it is the result of four months' unremitting labour, and to tell the truth I'm very proud of myself.

How are you getting on, my dear? How is life? Why do you write to me so little? Why don't you write anything about the others? Haven't you changed your surname yet? Haven't you got married to V.? How are things working out about your journey to the Murmansk pinewoods and the green forests?† Why do I have to find out about such interesting tourist trips from elsewhere at second hand? By the way, if you do go, thank them for the photograph of my loved one. And hurry up with the delivery of the return photo. Tell my 'official photographer', V., to send a portrait with flowers in it, where I don't look so thin. But what am I giving advice for? He has any number of pictures of me, only V. is too lazy to sort them out. I have asked him to send a couple here as well – girlfriends of mine who are about to go back home have requested some. But you know what our friend V. is like . . .

If you haven't received my thank-you letter yet, then let me thank you once again for all your trouble and for the parcel. Everything was done in the best possible way. I am very grateful. I have revived somewhat now, even put on a bit of weight, and have steered the offspring on to a homeward course as things should be. Thank you.

. . .

What can I say that will cheer you up a bit? How about

---

* *This is a letter sent from Siberia where the European part of the USSR is referred to as the 'West'.*
† *She means a trip to a camp to see one of their mutual friends, to the Zelyony Bor (Green Forest) settlement in the Murmansk region.*

the grand 'Bustarama' that Zukhra and I have started up? A 'Bustarama' is an exhibition of the busts of our hated bosses and overseers. And the story of how it started is as follows.

It had been raining without stopping for a week, so we hadn't transported any cement, not because the authorities were loath to send Zukhra and me out into the pouring rain, but because our cart has no covering. We actually spent the time in the very same rain, miserably helping out on the building-site, dragging wheelbarrows filled with bricks up wooden planks to the first floor. A filthy, soaking-wet job because there's no roof yet on the first floor, either. Then the rain stopped, we harnessed up our nag and went off to the cement store. But it had been leaking. And where water had dripped down from the roof on to the cement, splodges of concrete had formed, of the most varied shapes and sizes. We soon selected some of the most sculpturally detailed and used them to construct a dozen or so busts of our overseers. We pulled some cement berets down over their eyes, and scraped out stars on the berets ourselves. Right in the middle we placed 'bust and stomach of a camp commandant', a very impressive exhibit. With the aid of two pieces of iron we engraved something resembling faces on them and then we invited visitors to come and look round – those, of course, from whom we didn't expect any trouble: 'Would you like to visit a dissident art exhibition in the newly-opened inaugural Siberian Bustarama?' We assembled five or six of them who did and led them off to our storehouse during the lunch-break. Then there took place an interesting dialogue between my Zukhra and the artist Lilya M. Lilya looked at the busts and said: 'Hm, formalistic in the style of Ernst Neizvestny, though the authorities won't appreciate this, if they see it.'

'But this isn't a Moscow exhibition at the Manège, you know,' announces my well-educated pupil impertinently. 'We don't intend to invite the authorities.'

'Yes,' Lilya went on. 'Nikita Sergeyevich Khrushchev

was right when he condemned artistic decadence of this sort . . .'

'Well, he was a voluntarist, after all,' sighed Zukhra. 'What else could you expect from him . . . '

I was more or less dissolving with pride at my protégée's performance. After all, four months earlier you couldn't hear any ordinary words from her, just swearing.

But then we decided to destroy our exhibition for censorship reasons, and Zukhra drove our nag right through the busts: 'Just like a bulldozer!' Since then, whenever we get angry with the horse, we call it 'Bulldozer' or 'oppressor of the arts'.

Well, it's time to be rounding off. Pass my greetings on to all our friends both in the West and further West. By the way, I received a post card from Madrid recently – it seemingly slipped through by chance. Good, eh?

Kisses . . .

From camp – to a woman friend

Hello, my friend,

I received your batch of news and your new verse. Which is not very good. I might add. You're displaying the same ailment which I suffer from: endless elaboration of the same images. With me it's birds, gardens and butterflies; with you it's reservoirs. And they flow from one poem of yours to another. Perhaps this would be all right in a whole book. In fact, I suppose, it would definitely be good in a book. But when you read the poems with long periods in between it becomes irritating. The poem 'Addresses overseas . . . ' is good until the end of the stanza, so is 'Lifting the sea to your lips . . . ' And then it all gets mixed up . . . There's something there of the style of Kupriyanov and something of Cheigin.* What's this then, girl? You always used to sing your own songs. You've got completely unhinged. Write it all again, that's my advice. And now I'm going to moan at you again, although it is about something different.

I'm going crazy here, wondering why Tamasya, my most faithful correspondent, isn't writing to me, and it turns out that she is in hospital. And you didn't tell me anything about it. Shame on you! I do know about your quarrel, after all. Tamasya always was a weak and awkward person, given to odd bouts of good nature, but not very obliging. She has let down both of us. But when none of the others had any time, Tamasya always used to concern herself about us. And in here I always knew for certain that once a fortnight I would receive at least one letter from Tamasya. I cannot tell you how much it means and how important it is for there to be at least one person who is sure to write. And then suddenly she stopped writing, and I began to get genuinely worried. And it turns out that she is in hospital. Do put on some warm clothes and go to visit her. And on the way call in at her place, collect up my accumulated letters and take them to her. By the way, some of them contain my new poems, including one dedicated to you. That should give you an urge to get a move on.

Don't get cross with me for this antagonistic letter. I say everything out of love. You get trouble enough from us felons. And I need your letters very, very much. The big shame is that you never tell me any real details about anybody, just bare facts. And I do so want to visualize living people in your letters. By the way, why don't you tell me anything about K. and V.? Where are they now? Where are they being held?

God be with you, my dear. People tell me in their letters that you are kind, beautiful and always cheerful. Keep that way.

---

* Boris Kupriyanov and Pyotr Cheigin – Leningrad poets.

From camp – to a woman friend

My dear lost friend, where are you?

What happened? Did you stop off to see the BAM* and get stranded? There's nothing interesting there – just the same old people building it, convicts!

My camp-buddies remember you and think you are beautiful: 'It's a long time since we've seen anyone like her!' But they also say that you are a blubberer and my name has only to be mentioned for your eyes to fill up with salt water. I explained to them that you are an all-out dissident and an heroic one, but of a particular variety, not unlike a Roman statue – with its regulation fountain!

After your departure I experienced an hallucination. I was sitting beside the wooden barracks, warming myself in the sun and working out where your plane would be. When suddenly I could clearly hear the whistle and roar of a jet aircraft. What would one of those be doing near our compound, I wondered. Then my heart began to thump and my head went funny: that's it, I thought, I've started to have hallucinations. I'm going mad. And then around the corner rolled an enormous tractor with a diesel engine – that was what had been whistling and roaring like an aeroplane . . . Some hallucination! They were bringing coal to the compound (our baths hadn't been working for the past two months for want of the stuff). Then some prisoners appeared with shovels and much swearing and set about unloading the trailer. I calmed down, having convinced myself that I wasn't going mad. How could I go mad in any case with enough friends not just for my own little

---

* The Baikal–Amur Railway, then in process of being constructed (translators' note).

fate, but for a good dozen of them. And there are so many things to be done – is that the time for madness?

Now there's one matter that I want to talk about with you. We've got a girl here who's on the way down – she's going blind. She is twenty-six years old, has a little daughter in the children's home and nobody else in the whole world. They're not giving her any treatment and don't intend to, because the loss of her sight began in the prison in Irkutsk during her investigation – you know their methods . . . And that's why she's here – because of the illegal conduct of the investigation: they have buried the traces in the muddy depths of our river. She tried to protest against the beatings. Now we need to get her out of here. We've already been able to get something done ourselves, but now we need help from you. One bright and not too distant day we need a letter to arrive from Moscow (it has to be from Moscow!), addressed to the commandant of our camp, in which her friends, or better still – her distant relatives (after all, people are all distantly related to one another) show concern about the health of Lyuda Grigoryeva: what have the administration and the camp doctor done to save what remains of her sight? Now some facts and details about Lyuda.

She is Grigoryeva, Lyudmila Yakovlevna, aged twenty-six. She was first in a camp and then transferred to the construction-site of a chemical plant. In the hostel where she stayed, the murder of a young man was committed. They suspected that she knew one of the killers. The investigation was carried out by the head of the Sverdlov district of Irkutsk Investigation Department, one Captain Kutepov. It began in autumn 1976. In April 1977 Lyuda experienced the onset of almost total blindness. The murder investigation was closed, but to avoid any embarrassment she was sentenced for infringement of labour discipline at the construction-site and sent back to camp. She appealed to the authorities, then to the doctor – they promised her an operation, they promised to send her to a special hospital in

Leningrad, they have carried on promising up to this very moment. But at the same time they don't even arrange an initial appointment with an eye specialist for her and she has to carry on working at . . . the construction-site here. The girls take her by the hand up to the first floor, but then she can't get down by herself. She wanders about with her eyes staring up at the sky, feeling her way with her feet. Meanwhile her sight gets worse and worse. She's a proud girl and very bitter. She just damned the authorities and stopped asking for anything. And she has decided on a way out if her sight goes completely: suicide. This will suit everybody very well – except me and my friends. So you must ask questions about her, all right? And please do it quickly. Other inquiries on her behalf are already under way, and we want the attack to be concentrated. At the same time as you send off your letter of inquiry, send a card to Lyuda herself wishing her a happy birthday. Then we'll know that your letter is on its way. In the card you might mention her eyes again and ask if you can help.

My dear, I know very well that the troubles of my poor fellow-prisoners are of little concern to most people. I try to cope independently and not bother anybody with them, and in the majority of cases I must say I manage quite successfully. But in Lyuda's case I am in a great hurry; every day is valuable for her: she is dragging around wheelbarrows full of bricks and mortar, and even with ordinary short sight that activity isn't to be recommended. She has to climb up and down wooden ladders without hand rails both indoors and out, from which she could plunge head first at any moment – with the wheelbarrow on top of her, instantly sparing the authorities from having to resolve the problem. All in all, she absolutely must be helped. Forgive me for adding to your burdens. But when *you* get put into prison (and believe me, they *will* do it) I promise to write you a whole letter every day as a quid pro quo. Can you imagine the bliss?

My dear, I thank you once again for everything, *for*

everything! Greetings to all our friends wherever they may be, at home, in the West and in the camps, and don't you do any more weeping. No more tears wetting my barbed wire, it's rusty enough already.

as they say here. Goodbye for now, my treasure. Write to all of us who are in gaol – we all love you very much.

Kisses . . .

From exile – to friends in the West

. . . O, Kafka, Kafka, where are you? Even your imagination would lack the power to invent a situation like this. The inhabitants of the next village are afraid to talk to me. They take fright at my very appearance. Even the children who petted my dog were summoned to the police station for questioning. The situation is so utterly absurd that I don't know whether to laugh or cry . . .

At night you have to fight off the drunks who behave like swine. There's one wash-basin for the whole hut. The rats darting about are so enormous that just looking at them gives me nightmares.

I am completely alone, deprived of friends, even of people simply to talk to, and there is no one to help in difficulty or illness. I am alone in my tiny little room, my fortress – which serves as bedroom, kitchen, lavatory, bathroom and entrance hall all at the same time. I don't have the words to describe how utterly awful my life is here.

I am as weak as any human creature could be. I weep with frustration at the pointlessness of my existence here. This senselessness is the chief cause of my sufferings. Only the awareness that I have helped Jews leave the USSR gives me any strength or satisfaction.

From exile – to a woman friend in the West

My dear friend,

I received the books which you sent from England, the tights and the marvellous postcards and, at last, I have received your letter.

I am very glad for you, for your success. Many, many congratulations! Try to be even bolder! And maybe, God willing, I shall also hold your book in my hands, maybe I shall find joy in your company.

Your letter is the only light in this dark phase of my life. At the moment I am on a medical certificate, but I already feel better, I have begun to wander around the house, and I have time, so I ought to use it and write, but . . . writing doesn't come.

Forgive me for not being able to pull myself together and write to you sensibly but, you must agree, it is in any case a very difficult thing to lose a dog, and in my position, when he was both friend and comrade and protector, it is especially difficult. And they killed him. He died on the strip of felt in front of the bed on the night of 14–15 October. And ever since then, when I think of his huge brown eyes begging for help, I break into uncontrollable tears. I tried to help, but they had attacked him with a knife, it seems, right in the heart. There was nothing I could do. And so he died, staring at me, a huge, healthy, handsome dog. All night I sat over him, hoping that he would come back to life. But miracles don't happen. I am now getting used to living without him. Already the drunks are beginning to wander around the outside of the house at night, and soon they'll be trying to get in. This is what used to happen before Rex. He saw them off and provided me with two whole years' security. Now I am even afraid that they will steal the firewood. Well, there you are. That's life without Rex for you.

My dear, forgive me, but absolutely nothing comes into my head. It was good weather first thing, but now there's a gale raging. The wind is blowing and howling, picking up the dust and rubbish. I expect it will snow tonight. By the way, for the whole of those two years I was afraid that this would happen. And when I saw him there covered in blood, it wasn't even a surprise.

Well, that's all. I shan't trouble you any longer or torture myself with memories. Forgive me.

Write to me, your letters give me great joy. They help me realize that life does exist somewhere on the earth after all.

Fond kisses, my dear friend.

From exile – to a woman friend in the West

My treasure,

How pleased I am for you, even happy! May God bring you joy and happiness in marriage for the rest of your life. I haven't even bothered to congratulate you, but have begun with my blessing right away. I have only just received your letter, and it was like a ray of sunshine, warm, so warm in my cold, depressing, empty and dirty hut. I am answering right away while I am still happy, while I feel the desire to write, while my heart jumps, and only later shall I sink back into my reality.

Yes, you have earned it, you have earned happiness! I don't think that you need to pay any more for it. Have you forgotten what your life was like? What all our lives are like? If you have happiness – it can at least be for the rest of us. The better things go for you, the little bit warmer I feel. That marvellous photograph of yours is already shining down and warming me right now. Be happy!

But now to more prosaic questions.

. . .

In my present elated mood I have no desire at all to write about my life. That would immediately spoil everything and pull me out of the skies back down to earth. And I don't want that. I will say just one thing: that I still cry for Rex. I am not able to defend myself, I have lost hope. I have always believed in the power of the word, but no words have an effect on people who are drunk to the point of lunacy. And they're all like that. You need strength here, and I don't have it. Outside it is minus 35°. And this minus 35° is beginning to tell on me. And so I send you kisses, congratulations, my blessing, while I await your next letters sparkling with happiness, and as for me . . . I shall go and stoke up the stove, or rather fetch in some firewood first of all. It's already dark. It is December, after all . . .

From exile – to a woman friend

Greetings . . .

Well, that's it. B. finally telephoned me. For two and a half months my heart has been on tenterhooks, waiting for his call.

'Hello.'
'Hello.'
'Well, how are things going?'
'And how are you?'

That's all.

What was God up to when he took away my reason and allowed me to fall in love just before my trial and exile? I needed so much strength, and then I . . . We're all such fools, damn it, we dissident bohemians! How could I let myself indulge in such an excess of something – which is nearly extinct. I am talking about love.

Everyone is given a tiny drop of love, but we let it

suffocate us – and yet none of us can get enough of it. And you're just the same as I am, so there's no need for you to laugh at me. I still have one more trick though – to laugh at my own stupidity – so it's still not quite time for 'Alas! poor Yorick!'

And you know, it's probably all to the good, it's probably miraculous even that my greatest despair is that stupid conversation with B., and not the horrors of the past or those yet to come. Perhaps it is wrong of me to complain about the pain of exile, if I can still feel so much yearning as a woman?

Anyway, my poetry has awakened, begun to murmur, begun to spread its wings. I am writing, of course, without any kind of dedication to B. For him it was an episode, an adventure, and for me: a new cycle of poems. Do you think that this is the end of our relationship?

Besides, a woman should not have to worry about this sort of thing, it's not her function. Our business is 'how', and not 'what', am I not right, my dear? You must agree that there is nothing more loathsome than situations where we women are compelled to make and act upon a particular set of decisions, because independence is the very first desecration of femininity. May God preserve us from such misery.

Look how many stupid things I have already written to you, completely forgetting about your own troubles. My poor dear homeless friend, I know that things are a thousand times worse for you at the moment than they are for me. But then you must believe in yourself, trust yourself as you would your best friend. I trust you, after all. And, word of honour, you deserve to be trusted. It's so good when you can say to yourself: 'I know that I will never let anybody down,' and then you add the words, 'nor myself, either.' So stop worrying.

I am so glad that you have a friend at hand. I like him. Only don't imbibe atheism from him. You must never do that; you're a poet. Remember that he is a hero. People like that are necessary; after all, heroes lead the charge in difficult times. But what happens when times change? Heroes don't give you children, or songs, either. We must be proud of them and try to preserve their beauty for the future, in which they will remain just heroic figures from a difficult past. But we will live on through our poetry, our paintings, our music – everything which we are able to create, everything which is immortal. It is terrible and sinful to write with such lack of modesty, but it is true, after all.

Well, there you are. I have been avenged on B. at the same time for his ruthlessly polite conversation. What do you think? That one day I shall once again . . . Hm! I think that I have already written or said that somewhere . . . Well, for the next five years at least I'll be spared these peripheral anxieties and then old age will be just around the corner – and we'll begin to live!

That's all for now! Many kisses . . .

From exile – to friends

Natalenka,

I am writing one letter to you and Volodya between you. There's no point in wasting paper.

What has happened to our 'fellow-conspirators'? Have they managed to come through the whole business? I haven't had the faintest idea where to contact them, or else I should have written, the old scoundrels! But I haven't got any addresses, so I am dedicating some verse to them instead. I am sending it to you to copy and send on, and to put in my archives.

Back here, I'm afraid, there will be more police raids. I don't want to lose the last little morsels that I have.

I have developed a rather strange relationship with my

poetry: I can write something in the evening, and the next morning I don't recognize it – it doesn't seem to me mine, somehow. But perhaps it's simply so warped its own mother just can't recognize it? Things are a bit easier with prose. I am writing a story and a film script at the same time. The same old dissident crime story with shooting and singing. I am getting towards the end. Soon they'll all have shot each other, so that will be something for you to tap out again on your typewriter.

I am still depressed. I can't stand even looking at this town, and I wander around like a zombie. My position is very uncertain: they might let me go completely, they might toughen my sentence, or they might just leave me as I am. They have pulled me in three different directions and then just left me to wait. A very unbecoming pose. I think they must be perverted.

Natalenka, send me some face-cream and shampoo. Without these petty female distractions life becomes completely intolerable. My skin might be completely covered in blotches after prison, but I may as well look like a human being at some point at least. Send me them quickly, Natalenka!

And write to me, or else I shall mope and stop being fond of you. And who, except me, would be fond of someone as big and ungainly as you?

I send a kiss to your forehead – on tiptoe, of course. Write!

P.S. How is the third part of my diary getting on? I am waiting impatiently for a copy, so I can correct it. What will happen if I don't have time? You must type it out and mark the places which look doubtful to you. I may have written something carelessly. Mark them in pencil.

And don't you think I got hold of some marvellous writing-paper for my letters? So official!*

---

* The letter is written on an Interior Ministry interrogation form, not so much because of a shortage of paper, apparently, as out of bravado.

From exile – to a friend

Well, what a right idiot you are!

I wasn't asking for the kind of letter you have to force out of yourself or one dictated by my girlfriends, either!

I wanted you to write to me about the weather, the birds, of cabbages and kings, our friends, poetry and prose and about those other thousand and one things which we didn't have time to talk about together. I so wanted just to chat to you . . .

And what frightened you off, I can't begin to imagine. Believe me, I now genuinely regret that I pushed myself at you in this correspondence, I think my only excuse is the peculiar nature of my position. I may be a poor wretch, as they say, but I have my pride . . . And I certainly don't go in for female flightiness. Except the most innocent form of flirtation. That I enjoy and approve of. In women. But flirtatiousness in fighters for the rights of man does seem less than attractive. Naturally, I will release you from our correspondence. In addition, I am going to ask you not to ring me up here any more. I can't stand telephone conversations: there's always someone else, apart from us, taking part. Let us communicate telepathically, then at least the 'whole of Moscow' won't be privy to our supposed romance. I don't like people laughing at me at a distance – out of range. So I am about to smash an imaginary cup in front of you. Crash! Can you see the broken pieces?

But seriously: I am saying farewell to you until 1981 and then we'll see what God has in mind for us. 'A five-year sentence isn't life!' our fathers used to say in 1937, especially five years exile. Don't worry about me. I continue to survive; the authorities are keeping an eye on me. I feel that very strongly. And whenever we meet, it will be as friends. Greetings to the 'whole of Moscow', and here's to the end of their gossip about us!.

Yours sincerely . . .

To a woman friend – a few days after being released from camp

Greetings!

You wrote that trouble from the KGB and the militia would be awaiting me at home, as with all newly-released prisoners. Well, it can keep on waiting. 'On earth exists not happiness, but peace and freedom live,' wrote Pushkin, but then you assert that neither freedom nor peace exists at all, and that things have become quite terrible.

Oh brother, what a lie! They do exist. You should feel my aching feet – they're completely worn out, tramping around the taiga. And the freedom here! And the peace! And the flowers! And the birds!

Do you know what happiness is and where it is? It's when one set of troubles have ended and the others haven't yet begun – that moment in between, that's happiness. It is blissful. I have managed to arrest it by not going directly home from camp, but stopping off on the way with a girlfriend of mine who lives near Irkutsk. She got out of camp two months ahead of me and was very keen that I should visit her.

I have been happier over the last three days than I have ever been in my life. I have swum in happiness in the Angara, and this evening I shall be bathing in Lake Baikal. I shall be travelling across Baikal like that wandering fugitive in the song.

Three whole days I have spent in the taiga. How miraculous it is! It turns out to be radiant, translucent, gauzy. I have encountered a new animal – a ground-squirrel. It chirruped at me and followed me along the path for a long way, pretending to be scared – every now and again with a squeak of panic hurtling up a tree and peering down at me with beady eyes. And then, when I had walked on a few steps, it would scurry off through the bushes to catch me up. I think it liked me, too.

I have come across many unfamiliar flowers, marvellously beautiful and mysterious. I have been collecting lily bulbs and the roots of some other Siberian flowers for Mother's garden. She will now have a little Siberian patch. I'm bringing her three tiny pine trees as well. I don't know whether they will take or even if I'll succeed in getting them home.

Everything is so bright, mysterious and beautiful that I have been walking around, expecting at any moment to see some ginseng growing. But the question is: how do I recognize it? I know only that it is a member of the Aralia family, and there are any number of varieties of that here. I didn't get lost once and, as it says in that same song about Baikal, I was not 'once touched in the woods by that ravenous beast' – the mosquito.

In general, I am fine. The champagne can wait a while, it won't turn sour. And all my worries can stand by patiently as well – I'll catch up with them in the end, I always do.

Kisses . . .

Second Bundle

Letters to Husbands,
Children, Relatives

From remand prison – to parents and brother

Greetings my dearest ones!

You probably know already that I am in prison, that I was arrested on 20 November. Yes, it is going to be difficult for me now to justify myself, to prove anything with no family to support me, no friends. The witnesses are a militiaman and the official civilian eye-witnesses brought along for the house search. I'll tell you everything when you visit. If you manage to come, you must ask the investigator for a meeting with me. Everything depends on him. He can permit a meeting even before the trial.

For the investigation itself they take me to a preliminary detention cell in a small prison attached to the local militia headquarters in the town of A., but at other times I am in prison in the town of V.

I have already been in gaol for twelve days, and I am still unable to reconcile myself to the whole injustice of it. I recall the words of one KGB man – 'You won't be forgetting me in a hurry!' – and I certainly haven't. He's probably still smirking up his sleeve. But never mind, with God's help I'll be able to tread the path once again. He will give me the strength to survive this second sentence as well, for what will probably be five or six years. Yet I could have stayed free, you know. All I needed to do was utter a single word. But no, it's better for me to do time. I'll be of more use in a camp, perhaps. It's hard, but I'm not the first, after all. It's a pity, I wasn't free for very long, I hadn't regained enough strength. I must kneel down and keep on saying over and over again, 'God, give me strength.' Pray for me. It's becoming easier, but I shall need strength. Without God's help nothing will turn out right. I think of Olya: she managed to survive eight years, and I shall, too. I am twenty-four years old. Add another six and I'll be thirty. You can survive anything.

Please don't condemn me. I am not guilty of anything. They have been waiting here for me a long time. They let the cat out of the bag themselves. And now because of it all, the only thing I want to do is go *there* – to the Father. Perhaps I shouldn't say such things, but I would actually be glad to go.

Forgive me, this letter isn't turning out right; the tears are flowing. I used to be stronger once. But the most important thing is not to let them see my tears. They must only see me smiling – even though it isn't easy putting it on. Just one thing I ask: pray for me. Don't worry. I haven't said a word about anybody. Pass on my greetings to everyone.

Andrey, you must read the Word of God more often; help out at home. Clear things up yourself, don't let it all fall on Mum.

Mum and Dad, forgive me for causing you so much pain now and in the past, forgive me.

So we didn't manage to be photographed all together as a family, after all . . . But you could all have a photograph taken without me and then send it on.

The trial will be in February or March, and by spring I shall already be on my way to camp. There's no need to send me any money. I shall work to get enough to pay you for the journey to visit me . . .

Well, that's all, my dearest ones. I send you all a big kiss. God keep you. Goodbye,

Your G

From remand prison – to the family

My beloved family,

First of all I greet you in the name of our Lord Jesus Christ!

I often think about the love of God – how great it is after all. If only we could possess a small part of this love. How little of it we have for our oppressors. And yet God does love everyone. He doesn't choose, as we sometimes do.

So New Year has come and gone. Once again I wish you a Happy New Year and Happy Christmas!

I am still in gaol. I haven't been summoned at all. I last saw the investigator on 24 November.

On the dot of twelve the loud noise of fireworks began to erupt from the town, so that we knew it must be midnight. But at seven o'clock it had already reached midnight where you are, and I knew also that you would have greeted it on your knees. I joined in with your prayers. It is the third time I have greeted the New Year twice over in this way. I saved a piece of smoked sausage and an onion from my parcel, and as I am the only one to receive parcels and as there are four of us, I shared it with the others, which made everybody happy. That's the way I live.

They will probably be concluding my case soon, in January. I don't know how to deal with the lawyer. I understand now that it is not he who is my defence, but God.

I have got something up my sleeve as well, to make the case lean slightly towards me at least. But I realize that they simply, well, needed this case. They have forgotten that one of these days I shall walk back into freedom and tell everything . . .

It was a little bit difficult at the beginning. I was free for such a short time, after all, and there were so many friends I would have liked to have seen again after the first separation! Yes, and regain my strength a little, physically and spiritually. But now I have surrendered myself completely into God's hands, and He Himself has given me peace. I regret one thing: they have taken away my most valuable possession, given to me as a memento of someone: my Bible. It was beautiful, bound in leather and with a lock. They seized three notebooks of mine, too, and an album, a present from friends in Ussuriysk.

I am very worried about you, having had no news at all from you. How are you all? Is everybody still at home? I often dream about you. Pleasant dreams, it is true. Once I woke up in the middle of the night and couldn't get back to sleep. I was carried to you in my mind and counted back the number of hours. It was only nine o'clock on Friday evening where you were, so a prayer-meeting was taking place! And I felt so happy: they were praying at that very moment. Yes, your prayers are felt very strongly. After all, Christ Himself said: 'Pray for one another.' My dearest ones, if it were not for your prayers, we would be in a bad way, unable to hold out here.

How is the Samaritan circle going? Who is visiting the old ladies?

Don't worry about me. God is with me, after all. I have thought and experienced a great deal over the last six weeks. When I was at liberty I relaxed and in some ways became a passenger in the faith. I would sometimes forget that we must continue to proclaim Him to sinners. I'm afraid that, during those three months of freedom, I only once travelled to N.R. to speak to unbelievers. For most of the time I was content to be surrounded by loving friends in Christ. Everyone treats me well here. They laughed a bit at first when I knelt down to pray, but now they have got used to it, and the cell goes quiet if I'm praying. I thank the Lord that He is giving me the strength to endure. At first I was very hungry, but now, once more, I have very little appetite. My stomach has yet again entered the 'convict norm', as they say here . . .

I am preparing myself for the trial and after that the camp. How I long to breathe fresh air again as soon as possible. I wish I could write to you and receive letters from you unrestrictedly. At the moment I am living in a state of total ignorance. Oh, to hear a few words about you, about how Dad is.

The printers have already been released, it seems.* Fondest regards to them from me. Greetings to all our friends, especially our brethren. And also to our neighbours, although many of them will not sympathize with me this time and will believe the KGB lies.

God be with you until we meet.

Your G.

From camp – to her mother

Darling mother,

> Dearest, gentlest, one and only you
> Who alone always understands,
> Who alone, quietly, caringly
> Runs your hand over mine
> To ease the pain and insult,
> Instantly transforming the world into home.
> How sad that childhood is blinkered,
> That we only understand all this too late . . .

I have arrived at last. This will probably be the last

---

* *The 'printers' are workers for an underground publishing-house called 'The Christian' who would issue in secret the Bible and other Christian literature. From time to time the KGB investigates one of the many printing-houses and puts the 'printers' in gaol. It is one of these groups that the author has in mind.*

stage in my new, strange and not always comprehensible life. There is only one good thing: the thing I consider to be the most valuable in my life – faith in God – which has remained in my soul, despite all life's adventures. I cannot imagine life without God.

So here I am. This is not the end point, however, not the finale. It is simply that my journey at present is leading me through the 'valley of the shadow of death'. And in this valley the Devil with his onslaughts and temptations is attempting to destroy my soul, to bury the pure and lofty aspirations within me, to stifle my energy, to force me to become a grey, ordinary, mediocre Christian, deprived of the desire to act, if not wishing to completely recant. 'Be like everyone else! What's so special about you? You have a family, children . . . Direct your energy towards bringing up your children, creating a good, healthy family, become more sensible.' This is all – from *him*. But no, no, I won't! I don't want common sense, I don't want to be deceived! I want to live an expansive life, so that everything must be my concern.

But oh! how I want to be free . . . And I don't want it in order to rest, to change these tedious, spiritually arid surroundings, but to live the life of a real community, to do something for all.

But even if my life is like this until the end, then all the same I still do not want to worship the idol of prosperity, the idol of material interests. Here and now, in the camp, I already wish to learn to live above and beyond everyday circumstance, above the conditions which I find intolerable.

Your S.

To her husband – from transit prison

I have the chance to send you an uncensored letter. I am sitting at a table beneath a nightlight in a huge but not empty cell and I am writing.

I travel and travel. They always seem to be taking me to one place and then I'm off somewhere else. I remember the old Komsomol song:

> Irkutsk and Warsaw,
> Oryol and Kakhovka,
> Stages on a long journey.

Well, they have already taken me as far as Irkutsk, so what lies ahead of me – Warsaw, Oryol and Kakhovka? I still feel reasonably all right, but I often catch a chill. It's cold weather, autumn, and I haven't got the right clothes for this time of year. I gave Mum's warm shawl away to one of the women transit prisoners who really didn't have anything to wear at all.

Siberia is pretty frightening. All the crazy absurdities of European Russia flourish here and become even crazier. Take the situation here at the moment, for example. There are six of us in the cell. Four of them are being transferred tomorrow. In the evening – it was more convenient for the prison administration this way – they were obliged to give in their mattresses, bedclothes, mugs and spoons. We put the two mattresses that were left next to each other on the floor and let the four who are going away tomorrow sleep on them. My cell-mate and I are sitting at the table, meanwhile. She is reading and I am writing. The duty warder comes up to the door every other moment and yells through the wicket: 'Why don't you lie down and sleep? Do you want to go to the cooler?' We don't banish him to the cooler in return – we don't have the right – but we do tell him to go to another not very comfortable place, because there is nowhere for us to lie down and he can see this perfectly well: the frames of the bunks here are welded together out of iron bands, the floor is made of concrete and the cell itself is a semi-basement with the usual consequences which follow and flow from that: the floor is damp and there are cockroaches. 'Lie down on the floor,' yells our Cerberus in genuine fury. We snigger quietly in reply – it is really laughable, after all. Earlier in the day I had asked the warder in charge of our block: 'Could you tell me, please, why prisoners are deprived of their bedclothes the evening before they leave for transit?'

'So they don't get stolen,' was the reply.

'But what about the mattresses?'

'The mattresses, too . . . '

We're still laughing about it now – the idea of some poor sod of a convict taking it into her head to steal one of the local mattresses! It weighs no less than twenty kilogrammes as, quite apart from the tangled wadding, it contains a fair quantity of dirt, bedbugs and lice. It's true to say that, given time, the wadding and the dirt begin to spill out throught the holes in the rotten fibre, but who's going to need the mattress by then? God, what rubbish I am writing to you. It's because I already very much want to go to sleep . . .

How are our children? On 1 September I mentally got them all ready for school. I have met children of their age here, young lads aged between fourteen and sixteen, and in the same cell as me there were two girls from the children's colony, completely corrupted, of course, but still only children. Just imagine, before they went to sleep I used to tell them fairytales. I looked after them as well as I could. I used to comb the lice out of their hair.

I kiss you all.

From camp – to her husband and children

Greetings!

It's my birthday, so congratulations all round. If there is anything to be congratulated on, which I personally doubt. All the same, I am happy and I have even got some presents: there are the trees which I haven't seen for a whole year, there is the sun which is shining – for six months it hasn't crossed the Arctic Circle – there are all kinds of things crawling about the grass and trying to crawl up my sleeve – it's fantastic. I feel marvellous, as Odysseus must have done. I am in the I-Te-Ka,* and at home in Ithaca Papa-Penelope is bound to be burning holes in the carpet with his cigarette ash, and both Telemachus-sons will be too lazy to do their homework straight after school.

Little one, your bear is living under my pillow, he hasn't got lost! Your dear faces are also close at hand, my children: an old photograph from the village where you and I all look like Robin Hood's merry men. The little one with his head bandaged, the older one wearing Granddad's airman's helmet on his head and carrying a can in his hands – filled not with berries, but most likely with some explosive kind of mixture. Mum also looks good, dressed in a torn old shirt of Dad's for some reason, All in all, a 'very true-to-life photograph', as they say here in the compound.

Dear Papa, the lack of comfort here has given rise to a mass of unresolved and somewhat capricious problems. I am trying to settle in as comfortably as I can, and I need your help in this. At the moment I am allowed one parcel weighing one kilogramme every six months. And I've got

---

* *A play on words. ITK is short for Corrective Labour Colony.*

enough requirements for a hundred times that, by God! But would you believe it, the problem of a piece of soap troubles me infinitely more today than the problems of peace and socialism. The only things which you can send in any quantity are stationery items, such as envelopes, postcards, paper and stamps. But please send paper good enough for me to be able to draw on it as well. You can also put needles in with your letters, safety-pins, hair-clips, razor-blades, biro refills. They'll either take them out, or let them through, depending on how the mood takes them. But certainly, it's very difficult living without a needle. As far as food is concerned you can send anything apart from sugar, chocolate, salami and delicatessen products, of course. There's no point in sending tins – they take up too much weight. I'm dying for some sweets, as there's hardly anything with sugar here. If you have enough space, or rather weight, left over, then put some sweets into the parcel, the most sugary ones you can find.

Now the most important things. A bar of toilet soap and some baby soap so that I can wash both myself and my clothes. At the moment I wash my undies with my last piece of coconut-oil soap, which is not just indulgent on my part, but nothing short of criminal. There's no choice, though, because I have no other soap, and don't expect to have any. I also need a comb. I lost mine in transit prison No. 11, and I had looked after it so well. But I am not Lorelei who can comb her hair with a gnawed-at herring-bone, so there's no way I can do without a comb! I must have some cream for my face and hands, and also some very light lipstick. No, Papa, it's not flightiness on my part, but because the winds here are the sort that dry up and crack your lips, unless you keep them greased. Natasha knows the cream I like. You'll have to send her round the shops.

I have already gone too far, I think, and yet there are still some necessary and essential items which I need: warm socks and gloves, and long knickers. And also some slippers because mine wore out completely while I was in transit and my shoes got stolen. Papa, you can get enormous velveteen ones with rubber soles which would ruin the look of even Brigitte Bardot's legs. They're exactly what I need. People say they're the most durable sort. Get me size 35 so that I can put them on over woollen socks – there's a draught over all the floors in the huts. So that's dealt with all the most important things, I think. Put them together so that they comply with my weight category. Our corpulent friend will help you. She is the guardian of one of the prisoners and is already bound to be getting a parcel ready for the New Year. Consult her.

Well, that's all for now, my darlings. I send kisses to you all. Give everybody my greetings. Kiss Grandmother and Grandfather for me. Put their minds at rest. Tell them that I am healthy and even in good spirits. It's true, after all.

Don't miss me too much, but then don't forget me, either!

Mama.

A letter to her husband from camp

. . . Well, so the idiot's dream was fulfilled. No, the Idiot's, Prince Myshkin's! How I celebrated Cheka Day!

Imagine a wooden hut and the following scene. The temperature in the hall and on stage is below zero. Outside it is about minus 40°. Seated in the hall at a distance, wrapped up in shawls with just one ear showing, are my friends. On stage, amid antique white marble columns with ionic capitals (made out of washing-line and cardboard) are those beauties, the muses of Poetry. Seventeen young maidens in long black skirts and white lace blouses (the skirts are made from black mattress covers, the lace – from bandages). I am in the middle in the role of hostess of a

Petersburg literary salon. I am wearing a black dress (we found it in the clubhouse; it's made of lining material, but from a distance it looks brilliant!), with a large piqué collar à la Mary Queen of Scots. And a hairstyle to match. A friend of mine said to me at the end of the evening: 'You were poetry itself, even though a little emaciated.'

I carry on a conversation about poetry and poets, and my girls (some of them getting on for forty) read verse by Blok, Bryusov, Esenin. We didn't avoid the Soviets, either: Gamzatov, Rozhdestvensky. (We didn't even spare ourselves Asadov.) Though, in general, the choice was not random: from Rozhdestvensky we chose the poem: 'They killed the lad, just like that . . . ', there was a reading from Musa Dzhalil's *Moabit Notebooks*, and one girl read a poem about children in Auschwitz ('Men tortured children . . .' Who wrote it, do you know? It was read as anomymous, but people were crying in the hall.)* I was master of ceremonies; the girls did the readings, and towards the end I myself read – from Osip Mandelstam. And beforehand I spoke about him, about his life and his end. And I finished my story with the following words: I know a lot about Osip Emilyevich, this is thanks to his widow, Nadezhda Yakovlenvna (then I told the story of her memoirs). But no one – neither I, nor admirers of his poetry, nor his widow – know one thing: how and when he died, where he is buried. Sometimes I look at our Red Mountain and think: 'He's up there, perhaps.' (Red mountain is the hill where the camp cemetery is; there's a good view of it from the compound.) After this I read his poems: 'For the thunderous valour of ages to come . . . ', 'Aleksandr Gertsevich' and, of course, 'I have returned to my city . . . ' It didn't finish without tears – in the tone of my voice as far as I was concerned, on people's cheeks in the hall. And that was the end of our evening entertainment.

The next morning some of the prisoners tried to catch

---

* *It is a poem by Naum Korzhavin, now living in the USA*

66

me in the dining-room and at work and asked me to tell them something else about Mandelstam. And they were very excited about the prospect of more evenings like that one. I didn't know what to say because during the poetry readings I had occasionally glimpsed suspicious looks on the faces of our 'half-wits' out of the corner of my eye. They're bound to tell on us and explain everything to the authorities! The deputy governor looked in at the club-house in the middle of the performance, listened in a frozen way for five minutes or so, and then went off. There hasn't been any comeback from him so far. But then he's not as dangerous as the 'half-wits'. 'Kings are less ruthless than the generals who serve them . . . '

Send me some more poems by Mandelstam. Gather your patience and try to copy some out of my *samizdat* book.

And now I wish you all a Happy New Year – a year when Zhenya and Vadim will be returning from the camps is already 'prosperous', already 'happy'. Pass on my good wishes to all our friends: I don't have enough cards or envelopes left to send to all those I would like to.

Kisses to you and everybody.

To her husband – from camp

My darling,

Pay attention to the date! Today is a happy, happy day for me. From today on I can begin to measure the time left not in years, but in months. I am into my last year, hurrah!

About your visit. I have thought about it and thought about it and come to a decision. It isn't worth your sinking into enormous debt just for three days. There's already less than a year to go, and I shall have to be patient. OK?

Everything is going perfectly all right for me. I am still working in the same place, on the construction-site. They offered me cleaner and easier work, but I had to say 'no' – the offer didn't feel right, the tone was wrong. The only bad thing is the cement dust, which you have to breathe from morning till night; you can feel it in your lungs. But I was able to inhale my fill of fresh air recently. For almost a whole month they drove us out into the fields to sow potatoes – just like they do with academics from the city. Being outside the camp is marvellous, although it's somewhat unpleasant marching along with sub-machine-guns trained on you.

I read the news about Arefyev with horror.*

So what really happened and how? A terrible death. Terrible, because it did not happen at home. NO LONGER at home and NOT YET at home. But it drives you mad to think of how many people have gone away! I have been trying to estimate how many of my old friends there will be left to meet me. It turns out that there will hardly be any. But on the other hand there will hardly be anyone left to accompany me, if I should suddenly decide to leave the country myself. Although I am scarcely likely to decide to now – my refusal has been paid for too dearly. That's another kind of 'refusenik' for you – not one who is refused permission to leave the country, but one who refuses the exit offered by the KGB. How many are there like us? Only myself, probably, fool that I am, and Sonechka S. If we can find another one, we'll be able to set up yet another underground union: 'Alliance-Defiance'. Do you like the sound of it?

What are your plans for the summer? Will you be able to get away anywhere? Or will you spend all summer hanging around in the town again? I haven't done badly for myself! How many summers is this I've spent in the fresh air? That's a joke, by the way, which only my fellow prisoners can appreciate. Recently a tiny bottle of perfume

---

* Aleksandr Arefyev, a Leningrad non-conformist artist. Emigrated to France and died in Paris in a car accident in 1978.

68

came into my hands. I sniffed and nearly blacked out – I was completely unprepared for it after the stench of the camp. Then the old carthorse which carries our water came up and began to brush her tail against me – only then did I get my normal breath back again.

There's no need to send any more envelopes. I moaned about you to my camp-buddies, and they have given me enough for the rest of my sentence. You could even ask them to get the plywood to build a plane with – to escape. They are the sort that can 'sort out' anything.

Well, many kisses. Write.

From camp – to her husband

Hello, darling!

Thank you for the photographs. They are marvellous.

I am glad that our son spent his holidays in the forest. Thank Lyova for me! I think the trip was beneficial in every respect, and the rest of the company was quite suitable. Convey my everlasting gratitude to the lion who tended my son. What a biblical situation!

Thank the artists for their gifts.

It is awful that you are having such terrible frosts and that Mother is feeling the cold so much. Can't you have her with you? Or buy her an electric fire?

I have terrible news. I have been robbed. They took absolutely everything, even the photographs. Stupid and pitiful thieves, somehow. What will happen to them now? The whole compound is searching for them, having taken umbrage on my behalf. To judge by the thieves' handiwork, they must be new at it. During the summer I scattered my bits and pieces in various locations around the bushes when I used to seek solitude and write, and nobody ever touched anything, although everybody knew my places. My heart grieves for the poor thieves, and for my lost property, too, because all they left me were the clothes I was standing up in. I didn't even have any spare stockings – they actually took all those darned and redarned pairs. Well, that's enough of that, we'll keep our feet warm somehow. The one good thing is that on the day of the theft it was extremely cold, and so I had put on all my warmest things, the result being that I still have them now. So try not to forget, when you are gathering things together for my next parcel, that I have got only one of anything now. And for goodness' sake, don't send me any more stupid things. Whose idea was it to send me that skimpy petticoat with the flowery pattern? When I get back I'll string it round his ears.

OK, all these are small potatoes. Let's get down to serious business.

Have you redone the room? What wallpaper do we have now? I would have preferred plain plaster and paint. But that would be too difficult for you. You can't even hammer a nail in properly, can you?

Kisses to you and all the monkeys. That's all for now!

From camp – to her sons

A VERY LONG LETTER TO MY SONS*

Hello, my little fledglings, fawns, rascals!
There are still no letters from you.
I am not worried: Granny writes
that things are all right at home
and that you are being quite good. I
am not worried, but I feel sad.
Every evening at seven o'clock they bring

---

* The letter is written on narrow strips of paper of the kind used for sealing gaps in windows: stuck together they measure more than a metre in length. No other paper was available, obviously.

the post to the hut.
Some of the criminal mothers who
only have one son each get two letters
at the same time from them.
And I have two, but get hardly any
letters from them at all. Every
evening at seven o'clock my mood is rattled,
and sitting out your time in camp is very
difficult if you are in a bad mood.
It's already too late for my elder son,
but I shall definitely pack you off, my
little one, for your silence – to pioneer camp
for the summer. You can at least
experience a little taste of camp happiness!
I shall also think of something
suitable for my elder son, of course:
I could construct a tiny cooler out of
our old refrigerator, for example.
Or I could boil him up a bucketful of
prison soup and force-feed him with it,
and then nail him up in the lavatory.
Write! or else I shall think of something
even better!!

   . . .

I was very happy to hear the news that
you had both been baptized. You are
Russian people, after all, and there is
no way you can live without the cross!
Such marvellous relatives have now joined
our family, too. Natalya and Aleksandr,
your godparents. It is very good, isn't
it? They were close to us in any case,
but now that it is official, it seems more
binding somehow. What was Sasha and
Olga's departure like? How did they feel
when they left? Were they tearful or
excited? What country do they intend to
settle in? Who do they want to live near to?
Who will meet them and where? In other

words, give me a description down to the
tiniest detail of their departure and their
plans. And what are your real plans for
the summer? If your father has any spare
money, then travel across here to pay me
a visit. I think that this summer
it would not be so exhausting, and it
might even be good for you. You could
see Siberia and go climbing in the hills.
They are quite high and picturesque,
although it would give me great pleasure
to wipe the whole picturesque scene off
the face of the earth – I am fed up with
the sight of them. And if you're very
lucky, you might see how your mother
handles a horse – like a real cowboy!
If we should ever move to the cursed
western West and become unemployed there,
I would go in for training horses. I would
find room for them all, lame and old!
If the authorities have planned for me
to learn something good while I am in camp,
then I have already succeeded. And one
more thing: one day I shall definitely
have a horse of my own, I swear by
Vorkuta and Siberia!
Children, did you not receive my Order
No. 1 for the House? Why aren't you
carrying it out? I send you lots and lots
of big kisses, my little cubs, and
am really looking forward to your letter.

                    Your disgraced mother

From camp – to her husband and sons

Laggard father and loathsome sons!

When will I get to see your faces, if only in a photograph? Or shall I summon you for a visit and draw your portraits here? Yes, that would probably be quicker and more reliable.

Things continue as normal. Or what counts as normal here, that is. All my thoughts lead towards one thing: breaking loose, breaking free, getting away from this damned place and sitting down at my desk to write poetry. And before I begin – a glass of champagne and an orange. That is the sum total, the whole sense of purpose of my life. I shall drink the champagne in small, slow, icy sips, I shall peel the orange very deliberately, and eat just one portion. And then I shall deftly roll a cigarette with home-made camp tobacco (I shall have to bring some with me, I don't expect I'll get any in Peter . . .) and I'll puff away, flicking the ash of memories on to the hem of a long, black evening-gown. Or should I keep on my stupid camp dress, the one with the 'label'? Ah, I am so thoughtless, I still haven't decided what I shall wear for my first evening at home . . . And until the moment when that crucially important question is decided, there is simply no point in my returning home. But then I do still have a year and three months in reserve, so there is no cause to get unduly worried. There will be time to think everything over without unnecessary haste. What to wear in the evening is a serious matter. Ask Dior, for example, he knows . . .

Yes, apropos of visits. No advance formalities are required from us here. There is a hotel where you can spend a couple of days, if there are no free visitors' rooms. Will you manage to get here in the summer? Perhaps we'd better see what happens in the meantime.

Boys! I am very much looking forward to getting your photos. I am already beginning to forget those mischievous mugs of yours. Sometimes I begin to wonder: 'Maybe it's two daughters I've got?' How can I prove to myself that I really do have two sons? I have no papers, no photographs and no letters, either, for the second week running . . .

How is Granny? How is her health? Why do you hardly write anything about her? You do at least pass on my greetings, I hope.

Well, many kisses, guys. I am waiting for details of those who have travelled so far away from us. Oh, dear God!

Well, goodbye.

Mother

From camp – to her son

My dear eldest boy,

How was your journey back from the visit? What were your impressions of this little health resort of mine?

I am still receiving compliments about you. You definitely caused a furore among our more youthful prisoners. The girls have been asking whether you enjoyed the evening serenade they arranged in your honour beneath the windows of the visiting-room? It nearly resulted in confinement in the SHIZO for the performers. Art is no more in harmony with the authorities here than anywhere else. Still, not a bad idea, was it – the whole ensemble climbing up on to the roof of the hut like that! In my opinion, you definitely have something to take pride in. So what message shall I pass on to the soloists and guitarists?

An intermission has been granted in this hell of ours: after a month with temperatures of 40° we are now having torrential rains. The cauldrons have cooled down, the sinners are resting. That is to say, they are not being driven into the fields to weed cabbages under the full blaze of the sun. I must remind you that one name for our valley is the 'Cauldron of Storms'. It is also knwon as Death Valley, but that is obviously folk geography and ad-libbing at its most outrageous . . .

I am still chewing on the edible joys of your visit and I remember its spiritual joys. What good, intelligent, happy children you are! How was I clever enough to give birth to and bring up such charming lads?

Son, I am envious of your success and have even begun to study English as a matter of urgency. But so far I have only learnt fifty words. Using cards, as you showed me. I carry them about in my pocket and look at them when I am at work.

Well, so long, my 'Prince-Imperial'! Devote yourself to your treasures (stamps) and scholarship (it'll come in handy), and don't forget to write to your disgraced sovereign mother.

Many kisses,

Mama

From camp – to her children

Greetings, children, great and small!

I send you my best wishes for the coming New Year. 'Coming' for me, that is; it will already have arrived for you by the time you receive this letter. I wish you the same things as I wish for myself: that this summer we shall meet at last and then go off somewhere all together, talking all the way to our hearts' content. And we shan't take anyone else with us, there'll only be all of you with your mama! During the winter you must all think of somewhere we could go. The whole world will be open to us – just imagine! The Baltic States – of course! The Black Sea – as often as you like! Or perhaps the Atlantic or the Adriatic? Anything can happen, everything is possible . . .

Thank you for your new verses. Is there a fashion now for these 'black ballads'? The only shame is that no one here is likely to appreciate them: they've got enough horrors of their own. After last year's amnesty there are only murderers and major state offenders left in the camp – and just the one political in the whole camp: me. What fine company for you! Their tales of murdered children make me see red. It's just as well that the authorities have such a humane attitude towards child-killers – they are being let out one by one on parole. It does make it easier for me to breathe, me, to whom this humane attitude does not extend. The sooner they're gone, the better!

Now I'll tell you an anecdote which my convict friends made up about me – based on truth:

'Our security officer got wind of the fact that our O. had written a long article about the camp. They searched and searched for it – and eventually found it. They opened the notebook, and on the first page they read: "I was brought to the camp one cold autumn. A strong wind was blowing that day, raising the dust and beginning to howl: Oo-oo-oo! OO-oo-oo! OO-oo-oo! Oo-oo-oo! Oo-oo-oo! Oo-oo-oo!, and so on for some thirty pages,

'O. is summoned to see the security officer.

' "What's all this never ending 'oo-oo-oo, oo-oo-oo', and so on?"

' "It wasn't me doing it, it was this lousy wind of yours."

'The article was sent off to the KGB and O. was shut in the cooler for defamation of Soviet reality.'

Witty friends I've got, don't you think?

Well, and how are things going? How is school? Are you helping Dad with the housework?

Kisses to you all, my little rabbits!

Third Bundle

Letters to a Lover

From camp – to her beloved in another camp

Darling! It's me, hello!

God, so we've survived to say 'hello'! How much water has passed under the bridge over the past year, and what water! I still don't know how our correspondence will work out, whether you will be able to answer me yourself, or whether you will have to do it through friends and relatives. But that isn't the important thing at the moment. What is important is that at last I know your address, I know where you are. I've lost count of how many letters I have written to be sent on to you from Leningrad. Have you received even one of them? At least now I am glad that I don't have to write 'into the blue' by way of your cautious relatives. I don't want to think or say anything bad about them; their fears are perfectly understandable, after all. They have so much behind them that we haven't even dreamed about. Thank God that it's not 1937 now . . . But all the same it sometimes makes me angry to think that I haven't had any news or word of you for so long, and all because of your relations' fear that you might be harmed by my letters. In fact, they seem to think generally that I am to blame for everything. How can they imagine that I could have directed your actions and held sway over you? Quite the opposite, after all. I was glad that, when I was with you, I could sometimes relax and not have to make every decision myself. You can't imagine what joy that was. Suddenly, instead of having to concentrate my mind on resolving some problem, I could simply turn my head towards you and give an enquiring look: 'What are we going to do?' Well! nobody guessed how arduous and unpleasant, how troublesome and difficult it was: being a 'strong woman'. Thank you for giving me vulnerability.

In every letter I write I tell you that I know all the

reasons why you and O. acted as you did: taking responsibility for everything, but revealing it all at the investigation. At first, I admit, I was angry, hurt, bewildered: 'How could they do it? Could they really have got cold feet and made a deal?' Then I realized that in return for this they had promised you that N. and I would go free. My poor cavaliers! They tricked you, of course, they could do nothing else. It's always the same: we plan our moves like a game of chess, and they play 'cheat' with us. Using marked cards to boot! But believe me: I don't blame you in the slightest, whatever the disappointed dissidents may say. To me you are still the same steadfast, strong, proud man, head and shoulders above everyone else I have ever known in this life. And as for allowing yourself to be tricked, well, it's only honest, upright people who are the victims of trickery. It never happens to villains. Never mind, my love, we'll survive it all and live to forget it. Ah, if only I could receive a letter from you soon! I've already forgotten what your handwriting looks like.

In my mind I keep on visualizing our two farewells – on 12 September and 29 December. You, too, I know. N. told me that the day after I went away you couldn't stop worrying, thinking that something bad was going to happen and blaming yourself: 'How could we let her go off alone? Where is she now?' But I know something else as well, that N. couldn't have told me. Do you remember, when you were taking me to the railway station, we stood on the platform in the Metro, waiting for a train? You were looking at me silently and suddenly said: 'How small you are . . . ' And I realized that you were seeing me at that moment through the wrong end of the binoculars – a long, long way away, and quite small. I didn't say anything in reply because I felt a lump in my throat. I realized myself that we wouldn't see each other any more, that I was going away from you for ever, and not simply leaving for a two-week holiday.

And then there was something else (I wrote about it in

almost every letter; this is perhaps the tenth time I am writing this, but it seems to me to be so important to us – these are our last shared memories, after all, and they are all we are going to be left with now for a long time). You and I were already standing by the train, when V. came up to us. I was very glad that the two of you were there, otherwise I might have thrown my arms around your neck at the last minute and not have gone off anywhere (I am such a fool, that's exactly what I should have done! They could have arrested us together the next day. Alone, on a train, at night – it didn't feel very cheerful, you know.) Then, a minute or so before the train was due to leave, standing in the corridor by the window, looking at you and V., suddenly there was a great downpour of rain, so heavy that I couldn't see your faces beyond the streams of water. All I could make out were two tall, dim silhouettes. And the train began to move.

And it carried on like this. I was lying on the top bunk to try and get to sleep as quickly as possible, to forget about everything and not feel the separation. Below me was a group of young people, boys and girls – tourists. They asked me if I was asleep and whether I would have any objection if they switched on the radio. I said, 'No. Carry on.' And on the radio someone was singing Bella Akhmadulina's song about friends:

> How many countless years along my street
> Have footsteps echoed – farewell steps of friends.
> The dark beyond the window-panes acclaims
> This gradual departure of my friends.

My heart seemed to stop beating. I listened, not breathing, every muscle tensed, and I realized that the song was about us. Here are the last lines:

> And yet one day out from the gloomy dark,
> Out from the ignorant brightness of the past,

Will re-emerge and once again dissolve
The fair and radiant faces of my friends.

Then the radio gave a crackle and went into eternal
silence, and however much the boys below tried fiddling
with the knob, they couldn't get one more sound out of it.
I was weeping and cried myself to sleep. But during the
night I woke up, hearing through the silence the sound of
boots – they had come to get me . . . Well, there's no point
in telling any more.

But what a meeting we had on 29 December! You can't
imagine how much of an effort it was for me to succeed in
getting you brought to court to witness my performance. I
wrote no fewer than eight official requests and at last got
my way. I insisted that I had some very important questions to put to you and that a great deal would depend on
the answers you gave. And do you remember what the
question was that I did put to you: 'How are you feeling?'
You had lost weight and looked very pale, but you were
calm and smiled at everyone. At me most of all, of course!
There's only one thing I am sorry about. Your parents
didn't believe that I would manage to pull it off and didn't
come to my performance – so they didn't get to see you.
And when they were taking me away again – for good this
time! – I got up and walked over to the barrier so I could
see you as close and for as long as possible. And then there
was a yell: 'Sit down on your seat and don't get up without
permission!' You looked round when you heard this, and
thanks to that yell our eyes were able to meet once again.
You see how I remember everything down to the smallest
detail. You, too. Am I right?

I fold you in my arms, my darling, and from this great
distance press myself against you with all my heart. Don't
be at a loss for too long. I need to receive at least *one* letter
from you so much – after all I have already spent a year
in silence, talking to you only in my thoughts. I am so

looking forward to a letter, more than I ever looked forward even to a meeting with you before.

Oh God, what joy! At long last – the first letter from you! Hello, hello, hello, my darling!

I received your letter on 18 March and somehow knew that I would get it that day. During the lunch-break I left the sewing-workshop and sat down on a small log near the new hostel which is under construction.* It was a bright spring day, and birds were singing in the bushes on the other side of the fence. I was very tired and sad, as I often am on bright spring days. And suddenly a feeling of joy sprang into my heart from somewhere or other. I searched my memory, but couldn't think of anything good that had happened over the previous few days which might have made me feel happy. So I listened to my inner self once again and realized that some great joy was awaiting me in the near future. And for the rest of the day until the evening I walked around in expectation of this happiness, trying not to talk to anyone so the feeling didn't spill out. I was holding myself like a glass of champagne. When the post arrived that evening, I was given two letters – one from Mama and one from T. I opened the envelope containing T's letter, and out of it fell a sheet of paper: 'My ray of sunshine, my darling girl, where are you?' Everything swam before my eyes. I snatched up the piece of paper and threw myself on to my bunk, clutching it to my breast. For a long time I lay like that, and then calmed down a little and began to read on. How terrible! You haven't received a single one of my letters over the last year and a half! But you and I are both made of stern stuff! We didn't give up in despair, but carried on writing and writing. 'It is so

---

* *i.e. camp hut. Correspondence between prisoners is forbidden, and so the author avoids making references to her camp in letters which are sent legally and subject to censorship.*

difficult, writing into the darkness, not hearing a reply . . .'
Yes, my darling, it is very difficult. But look! We've managed to get through! That is to say you have got through to me, and now I shall be writing literally every day via different people. There is also another way, unusual and quite original.

I have already learnt your letter off by heart, of course. Now, whatever happens around me or even *to* me, I am able to ignore any sounds and manage not to see anything even when my eyes are open – repeating, repeating *ad infinitum* the words of your letter.

Darling, you write as if you *had* received all my letters: you respond to all my thoughts and questions. Which means that you were hearing me all this time in your heart, that you knew what I was thinking and recalling. Yes, I, too, often remember the village – those were our happiest days. And that first evening kiss, in the mist surrounded by great trees – of course I remember it, too. The mist was so thick that all I could see were your eyes, even though we were standing quite close to each other. I even remember the smell of the rose-bay plant which was swaying by your shoulder and the cool droplets of mist on your skin.

And do you remember how I showed you all those herbs growing in the forest and you teased me by calling me a 'young witch'. Have you managed to remember the name of even one of the herbs? By the way, it wouldn't do any harm for you to remember something about stinging-nettles at least – they grow everywhere and contain a colossal amount of vitamins. Have you got any weeds growing under a fence anywhere round about? Dandelions, ribgrass, burdock – all these make marvellous vitamin salads! Please, I implore you, collect the herbs that you know and either make them into a salad, or chop them up into a soup. Do this whenever you can. I would love you even if you had no teeth, of course, but why not preserve your teeth and your health, if it is possible. I contracted scurvy during my first spring, and immediately lost two teeth. So now I'm forever munching some grass or other like a sheep, and this spring, touch wood, I seem to have got away without any ailment caused by lack of vitamins. Have you got any fir trees where you are? The best thing is to brew some tea from fresh pine needles. My darling, please, please, I beg you, even simply order you – look out for herbs!

Are you doing any drawing? Do you have anything to use apart from scraps of paper and ordinary pencils? I try to write the whole time, even when I don't feel in the mood. And I think you will like my new poetry even more than my previous writing. Do you remember how you kissed my hand because of my poetry, when I read it the first time for you at the F—skys' party? It is so marvellous that you love not only me, but my poetry as well. I shall tell you a secret: poetry is the thing which other men and my husband struggled against with all their might. It's always the same: first of all people fall in love with the poetess, and then they try to turn her into a domestic idiot chained to the kitchen. But anyway, it's true that I started to cook properly, isn't it? Do you know how I'm going to feed you when we live together? Aha, just you wait! Everyone will be jealous of you and ask to be invited to lunch. We surely will live together one day, won't we?

And what sort of food are you eating? Very bad? It's not easy here in the summer, because everything goes off in the heat. Most of the food here I simply just do not eat: it's better to go hungry than to be poisoned.

Look after yourself as far as possible, my darling!. I'll try to do the same – for you. I kiss you long and tenderly – as we did then in the mist. Tomorrow I shall write to you again. I shall write often, very often.

Your . . .

Hello, my ray of sunshine!

I received your long, enormously long letter written in

tiny handwriting over eight whole pages along with the drawings. Thank you *very* much! I revel in it like a favourite book; it is so long. While I am reading about one thing, I forget about another – and that is very good because you can reread it endlessly. Now, I am not going to write you a very long letter, but to make up for it I shall send you some of my new poetry. And then you can write back to say whether you like it or not.

You say that there can be no question of your making any friends where you are and that you are surprised that I have managed to do so here. Well, there's nothing surprising about it. Just remember, you were never very sociable after all, and I was always surrounded by a flock of friends. I find them easily here, too. Too trusting? Well, sometimes, perhaps, and they'll deceive me or do me a nasty turn. But so what? I do stupid things myself sometimes, and I excuse myself, don't I? And after all, the majority of my present friends haven't had my upbringing or education, nor have they had around them such wonderful, trustworthy friends as I had. And so I try to judge them by other standards, not by our own. Don't be angry with me for lecturing you. You have always had very high expectations of other people, as you have of yourself, of course. But you must try to be a little more tolerant. It cannot be that there is no spark of light at all in the people around you at the moment. Although ours is a pretty mixed bunch here, of course, and perhaps I am being unjust in reproaching you with lack of tolerance. It is simply that I really do not want you to be as lonely as you seem to say. I've got people I can have a laugh and a chat with, and even someone I can read your letters aloud to. People listen to me and are happy when I am. It is very important here to have somebody who is able not only to grieve with you, but also to be joyful on your behalf. I am not such an egotist that it makes me happy when I read the words you wrote: 'I now live only for your letters.' There is no need to live like that, my darling! And why have you given up drawing? Well, so what if they burnt your pictures. Mikhail Bulgakov's words: 'Manuscripts don't burn', apply to paintings as well. Of course, I understand that it was terribly difficult for you. Especially when you saw your mother's portrait in flames. I cried terribly when I came to that place in your letter, how could it be any other way? But all the same . . . Do you remember, I told you that my favourite artist is Piranesi? And do you know why I like him better than anyone? Certainly not because of his prints (apart from his prints I have never come across anything else by him, I don't even know whether there *is* anything else). Piranesi dreamt of building palaces, but they made him repair floodgates in Venice and restore old buildings. And he, yearning to be an architect, drew the palaces which he might have built. Not just plans, but the palaces themselves as if they had been constructed. And then his dearly beloved daughter fell ill. The doctor who swore to cure her could do nothing, and the little girl died. And then Piranesi in his anger and grief killed this doctor with a dagger. They put him in prison, and he spent ten years there. For the whole ten years he just drew – you can imagine what 'conditions' must have been like for him to have done this! And the result was the appearance of a series of prints entitled 'Carceri' or 'Prisons'. Some of these contain terrible, sad, hopeless things. But taken together they are proof of the fact that he never ceased to think and live creatively. And that is how you and I should behave: I should write poetry, and you should draw. And what does it matter that we are cold, hungry, depressed – let us draw and write about cold, hunger, depression. Anything but abandon that for which God created us. And then, if we manage to live this way, a time will come when we will thank fate for every day we have spent here. But only if we have devoted every single day to what is most important: creative work. And even if we weren't actually writing or drawing, at least we would be thinking about it, planning something, preparing ourselves to write or draw the next day. We must believe this in the very depths of our heart, my darling, my beloved. And then we will be able to endure everything and win not merely a moral victory, but a creative one as well.

And there's one other thing I have thought of, darling. When I send you my poetry, try to do illustrations for it. And when you send me your drawings, I shall try to compose verse for them. And so over the years that remain we shall be able to create a whole book. Can you imagine what an unusual book it will be, a book written by two authors divided by such a distance? I can already see it clearly in my mind's eye. Well, here are my poems for you. Think about them. And sharpen your pencils!

Forgive me for writing so little today about my love for you and for lecturing you all the time: I do it because I'm frightened for you. But my love for you is very strong, much stronger than it used to be. When I fall asleep, it is morning where you are, so now I am saying 'Good morning!' to you before drifting off. And sometimes I seem to hear you there, a long way off – already awake and thinking about me as well, before anything else. You must love me even more because the sun comes to you from my direction and because I also send you the night, to give you rest. You see how many good things I convey to you, not only letters! I send you incessant and infinite kisses. Try, at least at the very beginning and end of each day, to hear the sound of my kisses and of my love, as I fall asleep and awaken.

Your . . .

My darling,

Forgive me for not replying to you. I have already received two letters from you, and here I am only replying to the third where you seem to be already sliding from grumbling into despair. There are no reasons at all for you to despair. Nothing in particular has happened to me; I haven't been carried off anywhere, I have simply been ill with tonsillitis.

It was a fairly bad attack of tonsillitis with high fever, but I had to endure it on my feet: I didn't want to visit the camp doctor and ask to go into hospital. That's what I'm really afraid of, ending up there. Sometimes I have to go into the hospital quarters to visit someone – and it's a depressing sight. Women are already weakened by work and general conditions, and then added to that – illness. But the most frightening thing is it suddenly becomes possible to lie in bed, eat an almost normal diet (they even give you vitamins!), and you don't have to steel yourself from morning till night, to hold on, to struggle for life. Then the women grow weak, lose the will to live, and from that point it's not very long till early release – from the hospital quarters to the cemetery. That's why many of us follow the rule: under no circumstances, with no illness whatsoever, go to the doctor, but use your own resources to cure yourself. I cured myself with wild rosemary and by rinsing my throat with salt water. What a marvellous thing rosemary is! It really does help in nearly every case. I have other herbs in my 'green pharmacy' as well. Last winter during a search they took nearly everything away from me, so now I keep my 'green pharmacy' in a secret place.

Are you drinking tea made from pine needles as I ordered you to? Don't worry, it's not nearly as bitter and nasty as it seems at first – and you soon get accustomed to it. And if you add a bit more sugar . . . But then sugar is probably something that you've got even less of than I have. You have a much stricter regime, my poor darling. But then no regime is exactly heaven . . .

I would like to have written you a long letter, but I still haven't got much strength; sleep is helping me to get better anyway, and I sleep like a log.

It is only eight o'clock in the evening, but I am already in bed as it is Sunday and there's no one roaming round the huts, laying down the law – they're all busy drinking.

And my eyes are already closing, so I am going to kiss you, stuff the letter under my pillow and go off to sleep. Good night. Oh, I mean 'Good morning', darling – it is morning where you are, after all? No, it's still night there. My head is reeling and swaying like a poppy in a field, and I've got everything mixed up.

I kiss you, I kiss you, I kiss you.

It's not true, it's not true, it's not true!

It's not true that you're of no help to me, that you can't feed me or keep me warm or make me better. You just can't imagine how your letters helped me during my illness. They became the only reality I could inhabit and where I could recover from my delirium. Everything else around me seemed in my feverish state to be an even worse nightmare. And I would read your letters, as though taking a medicine I had complete faith in. They made me feel warm, too, of course.

Please don't get so worried about me. We women, even from the statistical point of view, are stronger and hardier than you men, so there! And how can a happy woman possibly die, a woman who is loved? I've never heard anything so stupid!

By the way, it is my firm belief that people die when they no longer wish to live. Or don't wish to particularly strongly. But *I* very much want to live, I want to return home and wait for you there. I often think about it. There I am, sitting and sewing something (for some reason I always dream about simple womanly work), and suddenly there's your ring at the door – four times. You know when you were already *there* and I was still at home, I never let anyone else ring four times, either N., or F. or V., the ones who had also previously used that special prearranged ring. Because N. once rang when I was asleep, and I heard the bell through my slumber. I leapt up only half-awake and, yelling out 'He's come back!' hurtled out of the room, tearing the door off its hinges and hurling it to the floor with a crash. My hands were trembling, the latch wouldn't give, and when the front door finally burst open, there was N., standing on the threshold. She looked at me and turned pale: 'Did you think it was . . . ' And from that day on neither she nor any of our friends has ever rung four times. Afterwards N. wrote a poem about it, containing something like the following:

> My brother, vision, love,
> In dreams I call you to me.
> And then from the door-bell resound four prearranged rings.
> I rush to the threshold –
> A guest stands there, no brother . . .
> And once again silence, once more the world is hushed . . .

I don't remember what comes next. But I shouldn't be thinking back to all this. You know, things are much better now than they were that autumn when we didn't know where the other one was or what was happening to each other and how it would all end. And then the following year and a half when it seemed that there was no way for us to get through to one another. Now we have our letters, our thread which you and I have stretched, one holding each end. It is terrible to think what would have happened to me if I hadn't had your letters! It wouldn't be an exaggeration to say that I live mainly through them. You must write to me more often for that reason, all right? And I'll do the same.

Well, goodbye for now.

Greetings to my favourite artist in the world!

I got your letter with the three drawings, and I was terribly pleased. Do you know that you have got a lot better as an artist? Once again I am convinced that you draw not with your hand but with the spirit. Now that you have matured spiritually, your drawings have matured too. And you complain . . . You like the poetry I am writing now more than my earlier verse, too, don't you? You have already written about that or something like it, but I don't miss a compliment and won't forget it.

Do you know which one I liked most of all? That little landscape with the cold sun on the hillside. It is so much like and at the same time quite unlike the view over the top of our fences: our own Siberian hills. It is a pity that nobody can come here and take a photograph of them to show you what I have been looking at day in day out for the last two years. Don't get too upset that you don't have the right conditions for sketching, that your drawings are confiscated, that your ink freezes up. True, my poetry doesn't get stolen – I know how to hide it like a magpie. But as far as everything else is concerned, it's just the same here. Sometimes your soul loses heart – and you can't write at all. All in all, the world which surrounds me here isn't the world of my poetry, as you must know yourself. I just can't imagine what I would write about, if you didn't exist, and your love.

Oh, what joy you gave me with your silly jealousy of V.! It came just at the right time! Yes, yes, of course V. was in love with me. Well, so what? He's not been the only one, thank God! What kind of poetess hasn't got someone or other in love with her the whole time? It's a kind of creative stimulus, if you like! But why did you come to the conclusion that I must have attributed anything other than statistical significance to it? Yes, I caught his gaze and his sighing – but then I folded them carefully away into my basket and carried on. And what business is it of mine that he's become famous for something or other over there or that the Western radio stations keep on talking about him? Perhaps our world isn't as important as the world of 'professional dissidents', but on the other hand it is easier to breathe in it and – I am quite certain of this! – more important things have been achieved in it. It's simply that now is the time for heroes, not for sages, and so those of us who can write, draw and compose music also have to become heroes, willy-nilly. But then you and I do understand what is happening after all, that we are being forced to do things at the moment quite outside our vocation. V., however, is one of those people who, when it is merely a matter of writing poetry, can do absolutely nothing, who can only come up with the goods in the time of the hero. God, how I would like to live in a world without heroes! And this, may I modestly remark, in spite of the fact that they have already managed to promote me to the rank of heroine! This doesn't warm my heart, however. Well, yes, I've digressed. Now what was it I wanted to say? Only that it is extremely delightful that you are jealous of me at this moment. Jealous of me as if it were a question of V. boldy courting me at some poetry evening, as if I were still floating about in a fabulous long skirt and layers of lace like I used to, as if there were nothing else for us to do except be jealous of one another and have scenes! Do you remember that time we were wandering around the Petrograd Side at night, and I became jealous of you and N.? I really made a scene, screaming and shouting at you not to follow me before I haughtily stomped off home. On the way I came to my senses, of course, realized that I had lost you for ever, burst into tears and resolved to kill myself, but when I got home, you were waiting for me in the entrance. And now, when you and I sit in captivity almost at opposite ends of the earth (well, at opposite ends of one sixth part of the earth at least) and our voices take a whole month to reach each other, and we are even distanced in time (when it's morning where you are, it is evening here), and seeing each other seems so infinitely distant and uncertain – now, we have no need to be jealous or doubtful of each other. After all, take away this love of ours and we would turn into the poorest people in the world. How many pairs of socks do you have, for example? A couple? And with heels which you've patched yourself, I bet. I have got one bra, and recently someone stole my toothbrush, and I'm very worried about whether I'll be able to get a new one in three weeks' time when our section is allowed to buy things. And to judge from the sketch which you made of me last year, you know exactly what a mess I look now – a tattered prisoner in big boots and a white shawl. So there you are: like this we have at last found one another.

But all the same, my darling, real life can be found where people are jealous of each other, have quarrels and make up and do a million stupid things. Oh! how I want to do stupid things, to be capricious, frivolous and happy! You men are swine for making the world as it is. We women would have made it cosier and happier, if we'd have had our way. A world in which people would have loved more, and not just fought each other and gone in for discoveries and exploits. Huh! your discoveries and exploits! We on the other hand can make a living person almost out of nothing – that's real discovery for you, that's creativity, that's an exploit! And all the same, your discoveries, your much vaunted progress (with its prisons, camps, atom bombs and I don't know what other male amusements) – all this comes from a hidden inferiority complex – you just can't give birth to a child, that's it!

There! I've been waffling on about completely the wrong thing. Forgive me. Farewell for now, keep loving me and be jealous more often.

Kisses, kisses, kisses.

. . . How amazing, my darling! Your dream, I mean. Your letter arrived two days ago, but I still can't get over it. Do you realize that you had an exact dream of our camp? Yesterday I got the draft copies of my letters to you out of their hiding-place and read them again – no, nowhere did I mention either the building-site, or the men from the adjacent compound. The point is that a month ago I was transferred from the laundry to work on the building-site. (The camps continue to grow along with Leninist democracy, they are expanding together . . .) We are constructing a new hospital building because there are so many sick people. They already occupy two huts (one general quarters and one for TB patients), so our administration decided to build more. And working alongside us are the same men who so surprised you in your dream: bricklayers, electricians, carpenters. At the moment we are at work on the first floor. There are no staircases and we really do walk along wooden planks and up ladders. In some places there are no ceilings, and moving along these planks, especially with a wheelbarrow and a clumsy partner, can be quite risky. But it wasn't a wheelbarrow full of bricks and mortar you were shifting, after all, it was just me, so probably everything turned out all right. Especially as I weigh significantly less than a wheelbarrow filled with concrete: only thirty-six kilos. I weighed myself recently in our refectory on the scales used for weighing potatoes; I don't think they would err towards exaggeration. Potatoes are a useful vegetable after all, and my fellow-convicts would certainly know what to do with the scales to get a few more of them. There's only one thing in your dream that I can't understand: why couldn't you manage to find a way out of this building? Wouldn't I have told you? Though perhaps I do understand! While you were carrying me, I had nothing else to do, so my head was probably snuggled by your ear and I was certainly not whispering what direction you should take, but much more important trifles about how I really loved you and how I had missed you. And how I *have* missed you! And the bit about spring was quite right, because the snow really has already melted here. We are a lot further south than you, after all, and when you are just beginning to see the sun, our snow is already disappearing. True, in the winter we have it as cold as you, but then you get some heat from the Gulf Stream after all, and here we get 40° both winter and summer for some reason, only one with a plus and the other with a minus sign. It sometimes drops as low as 50° below here, with a wind to boot. Brr! Still, what's the point of thinking about that now . . . Think of all the sun we are going to have before the next frosts!

You know, I can't begin to tell you how much I keep reliving that amazing dream of yours – it's as if you really have spent time here. The building-site is starting to seem the best place in the camp – he has been there, after all. You and I are either very stupid, or very happy. Which do you think? The second, in my opinion. And that's why I kiss you now as I must have kissed you in the dream. See you in the next one, my darling!

Hello, my dear grouser and grumbler!

You just don't appreciate me. That's what it is! Instead of being glad that I still write poetry even when I am ill, in the 'cooler', or in a lousy mood, you scold me for the hopeless melancholy of some of my verse. But don't you think that to describe the state of melancholy is already to overcome it? Genuine despair is when you can't write and you can't breathe. May God give us fewer of those moments. And the fact that on the anniversary of Valentin's death I remembered and wrote about it does not necessarily mean that I am thinking of dying myself. You say that I admire 'the refined attributes of death'. Aren't you ashamed to write such things to a weak, helpless, defenceless woman? And by the way, that portrait of you in front of the camp fence with a watchtower in the background isn't exactly optimistic either! But I don't get at you for depicting yourself as a monument of your own imaginary grave. In your portrait you look as gloomy as the Commendatore's statue on the opera stage. So there you are. Take that from me! To punish you I am sending another six poems written during this spring. One of them

– about an isolated tree fortress on a hill – requires eluci-
dation. The point is that last month they drove us out to
sow potatoes. We're not fed by the state like Luis Corvolan,
after all. We have to feed ourselves and even sow the
potatoes for the camp, our main food apart from rotten
fish. And so we were put into groups of five and escorted
by sub-machine-guns and guard-dogs to a distant field. We
had to walk five or six kilometres. For a normal person
that isn't very much. You and I used to walk greater
distances on our evening strolls. But here we had to walk
along in a column, to the shouting and swearing of escort
guards who for some reason are always bad-tempered.
When we left, the sun had only just risen and was trying
to penetrate the morning mist. The roads here are terrible;
there's usually no dust on them first thing in the morning,
the dew keeps it down. But not much later an enormous
dustcloud arose and enveloped our company, already grey
enough without that. 'There's only dust, dust, dust, dust
from beneath the marching boots . . . ' And suddenly I saw
ahead of me an isolated, round-topped hill, all green and
gold, and on top of it an enormous tree with a crown like
a sort of complete green castle-city. Towers, crenellated
walls, bridges and sharp-pointed roofs – that's how it
looked to me through the mist. I no longer noticed the
dust, and for the rest of the journey just stared over people's
heads at this tree on the hill. It was probably some ancient
cedar, to judge from its crenellated summit. I'm explaining
this to you in detail in case you accidentally come to the
conclusion that I have been transferred from this camp to
somewhere near Rome.

The poem about the pigeon needn't surprise you, either.
It's not an invention on my part. We really do have a
whole flock of pigeons living in an old wooden hut, or rather
in its loft. You should see how the prisoners, especially the
old and the infirm, love these not particularly beautiful
birds. What more can I say? They share their camp rations
with them, and that really means something. We've got

cats as well, and people love them, too. The prisoners, I mean – not the administration. Although we've got hordes of rats in the dining-room, the authorities still hunt our cats with a relentless persistence worthy of Jim Corbet, the legendary hunter of man-eating tigers. In just the same way they try to sniff out whether someone has planted an onion or some fennel in some corner of the camp, and if they find it, they mercilessly pull it out – 'It's against the rules!' Have you ever heard anything so stupid? If I were in charge, I would only let the prisoners do two things: look after the animals and work at market-gardening. But then, if I were in charge, there wouldn't be any prisoners at all. After all, seventy per cent of my friends here in the camp should be pardoned and released. But then what ought to be done with the thirty per cent who really should be isolated from others, murderers, for example? Have you ever thought about that? What would you offer instead? After all, we do know that the real criminals are those who have it in their blood – cruelty, the desire for violence, contempt for the life of another person. We don't need camps, that's clear. But what, then? Of course, most of them are as they are because of social problems. But what ought to be done with them all the same, where should they go? You can't *kill* them, after all! A murderer is a monster, a fiend, but if they are condemned to death, then ordinary people in whose name the sentence is passed, and the people whose duty it is to carry it out, the judges and hangmen, *they* become murderers as well, only much worse. Worse, because they act while in their right mind and according to the law. That's why I have never been able to find any scheme which would satisfy me from the ethical point of view.

And you know, I can recognize murderers right away. They have a kind of misty film over their eyes which makes even black eyes seem whitish. I have never once been wrong. No, I tell a lie. Once I was wrong. It was an old woman, Aunt Tanya as we used to call her. While drunk she had flung an alarm clock at her sister which struck her on the temple. She arrived in the camp and asked to be given the dirtiest and most degrading of jobs – cleaning out the latrines (the very thought of which makes my stomach heave). But then, you must know all about it yourself. So don't worry, I won't describe it. People who were remanded with her in prison at the same time say that she was convinced she would be sentenced to be shot. And when they gave her ten years in the camp, she went straight to her cell from the courthouse and tried to hang herself that night: she had condemned herself to death, you see. And she doesn't have that film over her eyes. Obviously because the murder really did happen by accident. She is consumed with grief to this day and keeps on repeating to everyone that she is worse than anyone else in the camp, that she is the most terrible of criminals, having murdered her one and only beloved sister. I would give Aunt Tanya a pardon, of course. Only she wouldn't pardon herself, that's the problem. And do you know what else she does? Because of her unhealthy work she receives half a litre of milk a day. The only people apart from her to get milk are the TB patients. They exchange their milk for tobacco and food, but Aunt Tanya gives hers to the sick and the starving. She doesn't drink it herself. That's a kind of self-punishment, too. I asked her one day whether she believed in God. She said she did, but that she didn't pray because 'God would shrink from my prayers'.

So there you are. I've told you a lot today about our life here. Why is it that you never write about yours? It would be interesting, after all . . .

Somehow I can't seem to manage to finish this letter. I just can't help chatting on and on to you. Can you imagine how we'll talk when we meet again? Day and night, I expect. Although during the night we'll have other things to do as well. Oh! but that's one thing we mustn't talk about! Sorry, I mentioned it by accident. You know, I have to try simply not to remember such things, or else I'd go mad. And it's sad. It's as if we're only shadows of ourselves, souls without bodies. Well, in that case I shall have to kiss your soul. Goodbye for now.

So summer is coming to an end, my darling. I received your letter with the yellow leaf from the birch tree in the camp and felt sad. The new winter will soon be here – my last one. Getting through it won't be easy, but then afterwards spring will come and then – home. If God preserves me, of course. No, don't get upset. It's not despair on my part, and fear even less. But we mustn't forget that everything lies in God's will. I want to believe that just as He has preserved us up to this moment, He will continue to preserve us in the future. For some reason or other we seem to be necessary to Him. Perhaps it is so that He can be necessary to us.

Have you ever wondered what the Lord must feel when he sees those who don't love Him, who don't know and don't want to know Him and who mock Him in every way possible, to boot? I often reflect on this here – the place itself disposes you to. So if God is love, and we are created in His image and likeness, would it not be right then to use our own feelings to judge God's? In the same way we grieve when some person doesn't love us, so He must grieve, only much more powerfully. I can't really imagine that His attitude towards atheists and sinners would be arrogant, proud, indignant and punitive. Even towards those who have betrayed Him, turned away from Him, renounced Him. Supposing you stopped loving me and left me. Would I respond by completely ceasing to love you? As a woman, of course, I would stop being in love with you right away. But I would continue to remember your radiant soul, because it once revealed itself to me in all its beauty, riches and goodness. Almost every person who loves feels like that. So could God love any less strongly than we do? Every soul is open to Him, and after all, every human soul must contain at least something of God Himself. It's just that sometimes we can't detect it, and sometimes the person himself doesn't know how much goodness there is within him. God knows everything and everybody, so how can He not love all His children, even the bad ones and the evil ones, the ugly ones and the coarse? And for this reason I am able to imagine neither Hell, nor any retribution generally. Perhaps the sinners will simply have to repeat the year, as lazy children do at school? Or rather, no they won't. That sounds too much like transmigration of souls; it isn't Christianity any more.

Don't get annoyed that I have begun straight away with philosophizing. It's obviously a response to your huge long letter about poetry last time. Yes, your idea is very interesting. And thank you for placing me in the 'organic species of poetry'. I feel that myself, too. If only because I can't remember a time when I did *not* write verse. It began with children's riddles, counting-rhymes, songs, then fairy stories which I invented for my friends and pretended I had read in some very old and rare book. For some reason I was ashamed to admit that I had thought up the rhymes and fairy stories myself. And what I was more proud of than anything else was the fact that nobody guessed they were my work. But then when I got married, I tried to give up writing – my husband secretly wanted his wife to be 'like everyone else's, normal!' And for three years I didn't write one line. I wrote nothing, nothing – then one day I sat down at a table and wrote down everything that was stored in my memory from these years of outward silence. The result was a whole book of poetry, including even a complete epic poem. You've read it – the one about the garden. And the fact that you attribute some of my poetry to the 'conceptual species' I also find flattering. One day I shall be old and wise, and at that point I shall metamorphose into that important and prestigious species of poet. If things work out.

I have received a letter from your relations. They seem

to have softened towards me. That's only thanks to you, of course. It's marvellous. I found it so insulting and depressing that they had no time for me.

In Peter it's already autumn, too. N. wrote that there has been a new exhibition. Unofficial autumn exhibitions seem to have become a tradition in Leningrad. The only sad thing is that it's all minus you and me, isn't it? Do you remember the exhibition at the Fyodorovs'? When Kostya had sent that children's roulette game from Vienna and everyone started to play it there and then in front of the pictures and bystanders, saying it was 'kinetic art'. And somebody had pinned a little white notice on the back of N.'s dress with the words 'Exhibit. Do not touch.' And she was sitting there with that self-important look of hers, putting on airs and never guessing that she was just an exhibit herself! Oh, the bitch! I am still jealous of her to this day! Don't you go on assuring me, please, that you never even think of her! Of course, I did poach you from her, but that doesn't stop me thinking she's a bitch! There's justice for you. My own special kind.

I'm jealous and I kiss you.

Hello, my darling.

Guess when and where I am writing to you? At night, sitting by a bonfire! No, I have not managed to break out. It's just that it has begun to get frosty at night and we are under orders to spend all night on the building-site, keeping an eye on the concrete. So the three of us light a bonfire and do what we want: my two fellow-convicts chat and tell each other jokes and I write letters to you by the light of the fire. It's so marvellous to spend a whole night almost by yourself without your other two hundred room-mates! Nobody snores, or groans in their sleep, or creeps along the rows of bunks, looking for something to steal – it's paradise. A peaceful paradise. Except for the dogs barking in the forbidden zone from time to time. But if you tell yourself it's the dogs in the next village barking, you can actually imagine that you're in the forest.

Do you remember that bonfire of ours on the shores of Lake Ladoga that we used to jump through? And how you got annoyed with me for accidentally pouring water over you from the bucket, and how you grabbed hold of me, carried me right out into the lake in my clothes and tried to submerge me? And how I stole your clothes in revenge and recklessly threw them into the water along with your boots. And then the two of us sat by the camp fire, teeth chattering, drying out all our clothing. We had a good time, didn't we? But all the same I still owe you one because it didn't work out fairly, even so. I only soaked your clothes, while you soaked my hair as well, and it didn't dry out completely till morning. So if I should strike you as being very stupid on occasion, my excuse will be that my mind caught a chill after that dousing in the cold waters of Lake Ladoga.

Darling, is it really possible that they might transfer you to the chemical plant? If that's the case, then of course I shall come and live with you. It doesn't matter that instead of furniture we'll only have wooden macaroni boxes. Just give me one of them and that will do nicely for writing poetry on. And I won't keep peeping over every minute to see what you're drawing. Will you let me have a packing-case? You won't begrudge it? Well, thank you very much. Let's just hope that this piece of luck really does work out. Only, darling, don't try to live on this hope. I have seen more than enough prisoners here who just live from one rumour of an amnesty to the next. They're not really living, but vegetating as they swing from hope to despair and back again. That's no life. You just live on in your own way, love me and write me letters, draw, write dissertations on art, and if everything does work out all right, then accept it with joy, but calmly. Because our situation means that the authorities on the ground could decide to free you, and then the telephone call from above simply orders the decision to be reversed. Well, what am I telling you all this for? You've got two months' more experience than me, so of course you understand it all yourself.

I kiss you and wish you a happy change of circumstance; something which I am afraid to even dream about myself for the moment. It's enough for me that you at least exist somewhere on this earth.

Happy New Year once again, my darling!

If you haven't received my two cards for this occasion, then I wish you the same things yet again: good health, both physical and mental, and I also want you to have me into the bargain. As well as new works, new ideas and new friends. But above all: happy changes of circumstance. May the New Year itself decide what changes – but please let them be happy ones.

Were you thinking about me on New Year's Eve, sending me good wishes? I sent you mine twice over – when twelve midnight struck here and when it did again for you eight hours later.

Say what you like, holidays are the saddest time of year in camp. Our girls let themselves go a bit this year and even organized a carnival. And there was dancing in the refectory. Just imagine, I actually danced a little too. Though I spent more time observing the gaiety of those whose whole conscious life has been the compound. Those who arrived in the camp aged fourteen or fifteen and are now twenty-five or even thirty years old. Some of them were set free for a short time and then imprisoned again, others have been in camp without a break from youth till old age, having lesbian affairs, living on vindictive camp intrigues. They enjoyed themselves heart and soul – they've got used to that way of celebrating. I feel terribly sorry for those women who have got husbands and children at home. They began to cry right at the start of New Year's Eve –

'And now Mum has just put the pies in the oven . . . And now the guests have begun to arrive . . . ' And as each hour passed, there were more and more tears, and by midnight there were hardly any dry eyes at all. Of course, I wept as well: I am a prisoner; nothing of prison is foreign to me. And then a small group of us made our way into the stoke-hole and drank tea. I read some of my own poetry and other people's aloud to my friends, and we quietly sang songs. We wished each other freedom and prayed that we would not be forgotten by those we love – all the customary things. We ate a cake. I can give you the recipe. Grind up some rusks, then mix it thoroughly first with margarine, then with jam. Put the whole mixture into a bowl and place it outside in the frost. Later transfer the frozen cake from the bowl on to a round cardboard box (I decorated it around the edges with a felt-tip pen) and sprinkle with biscuit crumbs. On top, you can place a sweet if you've got any, or even better – one sweet for each partaker. We only had one between us, but then it was a chocolate one. So our New Year's cake was very tasty. On the other hand, we will now be without margarine and jam for the whole of January, because the next opportunity to buy anything won't be till the end of the month. But what wouldn't you sacrifice for a holiday celebration!

I have received a whole pile of New Year cards from home and everywhere – even one from Rome (Fedya sent it). The postcard shows St Peter's Square and the pigeons. It's so strange to imagine Fedya in Rome! But how many of our friends have gone away, while you and I have been sitting out our time in our different corners. It's sad in one way, but from another point of view I felt freer and stronger somehow in the knowledge that Fedya is in Rome, Kostya is already in Texas, both Sashas are in Paris, and others are even further away, all over the place. How much stronger do we become, those of us who have remained, having friends all over the world! It's Africa where we don't have anybody, otherwise we've got a friend in every country – that's our life for you now. Something has given in the state of Denmark. What do you think?

Darling, haven't you ever thought that you and I might go away after all this is over? I sometimes get the feeling that, in order to overcome this weariness, it won't be enough to return to old friends in our beloved Petersburg. I sometimes wonder what Gena, for example, is doing on the Adriatic coast. I would find a large, flat rock, lie down on it like a lizard and spend whole days simply staring far out into the free, free sea. And this would go on for very many days until the weariness had left me completely and I once again actually wanted to move, to make merry, to work. And you would be sitting beside me and be looking, not at me, but also at the sea. And you would brush away the butterflies and dragonflies, so that they wouldn't disturb the wandering flow of thought about anything and everything, as I stared out into the distance.

Or I would do something else. I would like to walk as far as far could be down a shady, woodland path. Accompanied by you, but in silence. And during the day there would be only the sound of birds, and at night only silence. I have so missed silence! You, too, of course. I am still a gregarious sort of person, after all, whereas you have always been something of a loner. What's it like for you never to have a moment by yourself? You know, I sometimes remember my two months in solitary here with pleasure – no one apart from prison cockroaches! Even the gruel-ladlers didn't bother me at that point. Only the force-feeding – that was terrible. It makes my throat gag just to think of it. They stick this rubber worm down your throat, and you're writhing around like a worm yourself. And then all that food bursts back out of it like a fountain, though already mixed with blood. But that's enough. Why have I started remembering such a horrible thing? All right, so I did have to twist and turn like a worm in order to try to stand my ground. Even so, I didn't intend to write about my hunger-strike at all, but about how solitary confinement is less terrible than being in a block with two hundred different women, none of whom have anything in common with you – with nowhere else to go, either day or night. Although I am still fortunate in one respect: I somehow manage to become friends with them quite quickly. I immediately manage to divine what is good in them, what can put me on friendly terms. I really have managed to make many friends here whom I can trust completely and whom I can love. And I am very sorry for all of them, that's the main thing. Even the really tough and brutish thieves and cut-throats. But all the same, captivity is quite unsuitable for women, even completely bad ones. Men somehow find it easier to acclimatize to camps. Although this isn't true of you and me. It still seems that I find all this easier to bear than you for some reason, that you have a more vulnerable core. You are like a hedgehog: while you are all curled up in a ball, you are safe, but the moment you open out, the smallest needle can pierce you to death. Or is it just my Russian woman's soft-heartedness: 'She feels sorry for him, so she loves him.'

Well, on this note – saying that I love you and still feel a tiny bit sorry for you – I shall finish the letter. I hope that you will not reply by screaming Gorky's words out at me: 'Don't you dare humiliate a man with pity!'

I suddenly thought of the enthusiastic Gorky on the White Sea Canal, built by so many convicts. Brr . . .

I send you hard, hard kisses, embrace you with all my strength and believe that this year I shall be able to do this in reality. Happy New Year once again, my darling!

Hello, my beloved dreamer!

I received your drawing of our 'future home' – it made me laugh and feel sad at the same time. That high stone wall and the trees behind it, and the roses hanging down from it – they could be straight out of Aleksandr Blok's

Nightingale Garden. And the iron gate with the car in front of it . . . But do you know why your drawing made me feel sad? Because in all this I could clearly see that you are dreaming of peace, solitude, retreat from people: hence the high stone wall, and the iron gate, and the red car (it is easy to guess that the nearest town is too far to walk to . . .) No, my darling, life won't allow either of us to go and hide behind a stone wall. Even if you and I one day really were to go off somewhere, then where would we find such a haven where news wouldn't manage to reach us of someone at home being put into prison, of another being sentenced, of someone else being searched? Friends write to me that things have gone completely quiet among the artists in your absence, that many of them have gone away, and that the rest . . . Well, what is there to say? There's no point in judging anyone. A lot has happened to frighten people over the last few years. I fear that as soon as we return home, things will rain down on us with such ferocity that we'll have no time for quiet nooks. But how I would love one!

Do you remember those few days we spent on Lake Ladoga, when we didn't even think about or remember anything serious (except for our love – which is serious, I suppose)? I fear, my darling, that that was our last respite for many years to come. I am not worried about myself: I have learnt how to write poetry in the bus taking me to work, on the way to market to buy potatoes, in my cell and the cooler. So I shall be capable of being happy whether I am going to buy potatoes or signing some protest document. I am even happy here – you don't doubt that, do you? And as for happiness through material comforts and happiness through peace and quiet – they are scarcely for us, are they? Although it's sad, of course, infinitely sad. Do you remember the words of that poem?

> You'll order me to wear a flowing dress,
> To take a bunch of flowers in my hand, and
> In our new house, to promenade the room,

Across the copper-shiny, honey-coloured floorboards,
A scene for you to evoke. And then you'll draw
The flowers while I sit opposite, reading . . .

I won't remind you how the poem ends, otherwise I shall feel completely and utterly sad . . .

No, my darling, don't draw me any more quiet gardens and cosy cottages! But for this one – thank you.

You know, I am probably writing these rather melancholy words to you because I am depressed. The point is that one of our old women who was doing time for her son died yesterday. She just appeared to be old, though: in reality she was only about fifty. Her son was trying to defend her against the drunken father, but the father's head struck against something and it killed him. The mother took responsibility for everything. And now she's just died from pneumonia. Everybody liked her and felt sorry for her (and they don't often feel sorry for people here, as you well know). Usually no one even bothers to accompany the coffin as far as the camp gates when one of those who are 'released before their time' are being taken out of the compound, but this time people have been going around looking sad for two whole days. There are those, of course, who wouldn't be touched even by the death of their own mother – they go around the camp shouting, swearing, on the look out for sexual adventures and profit. It's horrible to watch. But then you feel sorry for them, too . . . No, I don't mean to say that 'society is to blame, they've fallen prey to their environment' – what's environment got to do with their carousing and thieving from Sunday through to Sunday, week in, week out? I am simply sorry for them, without any attempt at justification.

You know, I sometimes feel guilty towards them for something else. I am already thirty-six years old, my children have almost grown up, and I have a long and happy marriage behind me (a happy marriage which ended in a happy divorce, as my husband used to joke). But I am still able to love, my life was very full before the camp, it is full inwardly even now, and ahead of me are a lot of good, unknown, hopeful things – of this I am sure. And then I look at my companions who have lived the ordinary life of a Soviet woman: getting on – aged thirty; an old woman – aged forty-five. No spark in their eyes, although some of them begin to flash at the chance of profit or debauchery. The main dream of most of them is 'somehow to manage once their term is up'. Their fantasy is to get a residence permit in some town with good food supplies, to find work to entitle them to the permit, to be allocated a 'room of their own'. It makes your heart ache with sadness. Particularly today – because of this death yesterday.

Oh dear, what am I doing, darling? Forgive me. I shouldn't really have begun writing a letter at all today, given the mood I'm in. In my mind's eye I nestle into your shoulder and sob and weep. And you simply stroke my head and console me. I love you very much. I can't imagine what kind of life I would have lived here without you, especially on days of such desperate depression. Farewell, my darling, until the next letter.

Greetings, Loyal Hand, Friend of the Indians!

Yes, of course, I hear the sound of rivulets beneath the snow coming from your direction and I consent to roll up my wigwam and journey towards the West, closer to your encampment.

Oh, my darling, can there really be only two months to go? Time has begun to pass so slowly that I want to shout for help. I have sent off all my papers, poetry, absolutely everything to various places for safe keeping. I don't even have your letters with me! And you don't know what a loss this is to me, albeit a shortlived one. Before sending them off, though, I copied them all out again. So if one set is lost, there will still be a second one, in another town. My friends helped me copy them out and were always pleased when the orderly handed me a letter and would give me a meaningful smile. I don't understand what they were pleased about. After all, it meant work for them which they would have to do in secret, often after the signal for lights out, furtively, and they were pleased, the idiots . . .

I have sent off your drawings as well and now feel quite bereft. Could you send me something, please – you know, some farewell thing which I could then take out of the compound myself, something which they wouldn't take away from me. A small landscape, or something . . . Only without any watchtowers on the horizon. It's a pity that you don't write verse, because if you did, I could learn them off by heart and you would constantly be with me during these final days and hours. There, you see: it was a good idea of mine to be born a poet; you'll never forget the poetry which I dedicated to you. Am I right? You won't? Even if we were suddenly to part, even if later, when this present loneliness has ended, this loneliness in which it seems that there are only the two of us in the whole country, seeing and hearing nobody else, only each other, even if then you were suddenly to be diverted and carried away by, well . . . and so on, all the same, you won't forget my verse. They may steal your pictures and drawings from me, there may be a fire in the house or some house-search in our future life, but who can steal poetry from your memory? It may seem, at first glance, that pictures are something more material, substantial and that poetry, when you think about it, is merely sound and nothing else, almost like music – pure ephemerality. But, you see, it turns out that we actually create something more durable. Even the pyramids haven't outlasted us poets. Isn't the Gilgamesh story older than the pyramids?

I have written all this, and now I feel very sad. A new, future life is approaching. What will happen to us in it? What will we do? And, you know, I mourn for these years, I already mourn for them. It is as if something very dear is disappearing from our lives, something . . . joyful. I know that ahead of us is the joy of meeting, the joy of seeing you again, of talking to you face to face, of hearing your voice in actual life. But I feel infinitely sad for something that is already coming to an end with my sentence. Although I'd better touch wood – in case they pin another sentence on me! It's nonsense I'm writing. Pay no attention to it! It's just the result of the melancholy I have been feeling over the last few months. It's the usual thing. As the old hands say: 'The first five years are difficult, the next five are easier, but the last few days are the most difficult of all.' Only Vasily Shukhshin really understood this, I dare say. Do you remember his story when the village lad breaks out of camp two months before the end of his sentence because he so desperately wants to see his own village again? Ah! how I understand that boy now! I am absolutely fed up with it here. And how I want to fling myself on to the open grass! More than anything else, though, I want to have a decent wash. Now don't get ideas into your head! In general, I am clean, I look after myself. I have even learnt how to make shampoo by mixing caustic soda and household soap, and my hair is always shiny and springy in spite of the quality of the water and the miserable lack of it. The 'camp drought' is upon us again, and a bucketful of hot water is worth a packet of cigarettes. That's the kind of price we have to pay at our market! And with this one bucketful of water you have to wash your hair, and the rest of your body, and your underclothes. You always think that you've never washed yourself – or your underclothes – quite clean enough. That's why I would like to step into some ocean, as large and as pure as possible, and not emerge from it until my whole body and every bone in it crackled with cleanliness. Oh, what a fool I am, though, what a fool! Why am I tormenting you like this, you've still got so long to go . . . I'm sorry.

I can't write anything else for now, I've dried up. It's a funny feeling. I've already done everything I wanted to here and everything I was capable of, but for some reason they still won't let me go home. And it's time they did, it really is!

Do you know, as soon as I start dreaming of visiting you, my head begins to swim. When can I come? When I arrive home, I'll have to rush off straight away to get an internal passport. Without one of those they won't let me in to see you. Can you arrange a meeting in advance? And will they let me in to see you anyway? Here they don't let non-relations in at all, because there are only two rooms for meetings and there's a waiting-list for them, especially in the summer. But I hope that I'll be able to come and see you this summer.

Yes, I got another marvellous letter from your relations – accompanying your last letter where you write that your early release is being cancelled. I am not writing anything about that – what is there to say, after all? I hope that you weren't relying on it a great deal. It's not difficult to imagine how disappointed you were – I spent the whole day quite crestfallen myself, although, to tell the truth, I hadn't held out much hope. It happens all too rarely, and usually political prisoners have to see out the whole of their sentences. But there's nothing anyone can do about it. That's the kind of status we have – unlike the thieves . . .

I hug and kiss you – will I soon really be able to do it in the flesh?

Greetings, my darling.

God, where did you find such a marvellous Omar Khayyám saying? I wander around the compound like a shadow of myself, saying over and over again:

> In ocean depths concealed,
> The kernels ripen, shell-imprisoned.
> Now is the time, o pearls,
> For you to glimpse the light.

And I was grumbling at you for not writing poetry. Thank your father for this translation. Can you really remember not only your father's poetry, but even his translations? Well, in that case you certainly won't forget my poetry to the end of your life!

I keep wondering what you look like now, whether you have changed very much. They sent me a photograph of the portrait you painted of me and gave to my relatives last year – against the background of the prison. I was struck by how you had been able to divine the changes of my appearance: you even managed to draw in the wrinkles exactly where they have appeared, embellishing nothing, except the expression in my eyes. I'm sure I haven't got marvellously wise and bright eyes, that was you flattering me. But as for the wrinkles – yes, they are all in the right place. All the same, I shall try to be beautiful for you.

I told you the story once of how it came about that you fell in love with me, didn't I? Well, if not, now is the time. Listen.

A month after you appeared on the scene, when we had already become friends, I suddenly thought to myself: 'Why does he just keep on looking at me in that brotherly way? There's something wrong!' The fact that other people we had got to know took us for brother and sister pleased me, of course, but . . . As our unfavourite poet Mayakovsky said: 'We women are trollops and wagtails, all of us.' And then one evening I invited a few friends around, you and some other artists, and instead of my everlasting thread-bare jeans and my boring old sweater I put on a long velvet dress and put my hair up. And I might as well be completely honest about it – I went to town with the make-up, remorselessly using up a month's worth of expensive foreign cosmetics. That evening a cloth was carefully laid on the table to match my dress, candles were flickering, and appropriate background music was chosen – harpsichord. I made conversation with everyone in a soft, gentle voice, mentioning not a word either about my 'love' for Sofia

Vlasyevna,* or about our recent hunger-strike (the couple of kilogrammes lost during that period now came in very handy), and at the end of the evening managed to arrange for N. to ask me to sing Pasternak's 'Winter's Night'. That was when you finally swallowed the bait, my poor little carp, my defenceless little fish!

It's true, though. That's how it happened, isn't it? Well, I don't deny it, I don't deny that afterwards I fell head over heels in love with you, although at the beginning I was only trying to regulate the status quo of my little kingdom: i.e. please be at least a little bit in love with me! I must confess that in those days I used to love having someone around who was a little bit in love with me, just a tiny bit; not enough to be a burden, but someone I could be certain of, all the same. Who could have known that on this occasion I would fall for the bait myself? Otherwise I would just have gone on wearing my old sweater, and you wouldn't be writing to me now, across so many thousands of kilometres, about your love. You're a mercurial species, you men, that's all I have to say to you, darling!

My God, what are they doing to us women? Dear God, what is happening? After all, I would so like to spend my life sewing beautiful, dainty dresses for myself – I really enjoy sewing, embroidery, knitting – and giving birth to children one after the other, and writing poetry, clear simple verse for children and grown-up children. And better than anything, write fairy stories. Do you know that I have a whole book of rhyming fairytales which I show to no one – especially in these bleak times of ours! They would all burst out laughing! Instead I have to rush off to unofficial art exhibitions that are about to be smashed up, arrange hunger-strikes, tear myself away at any time of day or night and speed away to Moscow 'for the truth', that's to say, talk to the foreign correspondents. And I have

---

* *Sofya Vlasyevna – a humorous allegorical name based on the first syllables of the phrase 'Sovetskaya Vlast' (Soviet Power).*

to wear the most suitable clothes for such affairs and forego everything which has to be renounced in this country in order not to lose the most important things of all: freedom and honour. Inner freedom I mean, of course (and that's another paradox: in order to secure inner freedom you are bound to have to pay with external freedom, but I suppose we all knew that). And now? No, my darling court-painter, I have deceived you – these wrinkles will never be smoothed out, I know that. And what about my toes? Can you imagine what they look like now after wearing these damned boots? You see, they're the kind of boots that soldiers have to wear, privates in the infantry! I hold my head high – after all, my status obliges me to do so – but what about my shoulders, will they ever stop being hunched? And my hands? They have become quite swarthy, and the skin has gone thin and is furrowed with tiny wrinkles. Do you still remember the candles, the poetry, the song to words by Pasternak . . . We struggle for beauty in life and yet become ugly ourselves in the struggle. When you see me, you will be disappointed. Perhaps, what you love in me is the ghost of those happy days, and then this severe-looking female convict will appear before you . . . Try to have patience, and don't be disappointed right away, OK? Time will pass, and I will become very nice, peaceable, good-natured, quiet and cosy. We'll get things together!

And do you know what a distinguished-looking old man you will become? Oh, extremely striking! You'll look like some retired old sea captain, or perhaps not a proper captain, but a pirate. A pirate who has wearied of battles at sea, bought himself a little cottage in Holland overlooking a canal and grows tulips. And the most beautiful tulip of all you will name 'Star of the GULag' – in my honour. OK? And in exchange I shall embroider you in gold on velvet a copy of your camp insignia, and you will wear it on your best shirt, like a decoration.

It's nonsense I'm writing, isn't it? Pay no attention, and

just imagine that you and I are simply chatting away together; we have all the time in the world. After all, we have earned a bit of a rest, haven't we? I mean that your letters and mine have been an enormous mental labour, quite apart from anything else. I can admit now that sometimes writing to you has been agonizingly difficult for me: either I was ill, or it was simply a difficult day, full of all kinds of discomfort (some of them I will be able to tell you only when we meet, privately), sometimes it was difficult even to breathe, let alone write letters. But I tried to write to you in a way that wouldn't cause you grief, that wouldn't convey my feelings of depression and hopelessness – and you did the same too, I know. I even know exactly when you were feeling very low yourself and trying with all your strength to lend me support. That was when you would fill nearly all your letters, not with words, but with drawings. Or when you would suddenly launch into lengthy disquisitions about the fortunes of world art. I know you, after all, my friend, and it wasn't very difficult for me to divine that abstract argument helped you to disguise the fact that things were difficult for you. There was one month when you sent almost nothing but drawings, and then your father let slip in a letter the fact that you had had pneumonia. Do you imagine that I will ever forget what you have done for me over these years? May God punish me with total amnesia if I should ever forget your great humanity – it is even greater than love itself, it is the Love which Christ speaks of. It is very strange for me to think sometimes that quite separately from this Love we also have between us the love of a man and woman. Shall we be able to combine these two levels in everyday life? Shall we succeed? But then, if *we* don't succeed, who will? How I love your soul, my friend! You can't even begin to imagine it, and I can't tell you, either. I keep saying, after all, that all I want to do is write poetry for children. But then, suddenly, something has resulted from our lives of such real importance that it is best not to refer to it at all. And so Scheherezade is coming to the end of what she is allowed to say (allowed by *you*, not by the censorship). I finish this letter with the tenderest and most grateful kiss and am passing it on via a reliable person for transmission to the other end of the world in what remains, may the Devil take it, this state of ours.

When you read this letter I shall already be home!!!

Greetings from here for the final time, my darling!

This is the last letter from your captive love! . . . God, tomorrow! Tomorrow morning I shall be walking away from here, leaving this Hell. First I shall walk, and then I shall fly. I shall be met, the air ticket is already booked and then – up, up and away – to home – and then: to you.

I don't know what to write. The last few days have been an awful turmoil. The local officials have caused me a pile of problems, of course, which I can't bring myself to write about now – I'll tell you all about it later. But the fact that tomorrow I shall walk out of the compound gates along with the other women is all thanks to my faithful friends. In short, nearly every day there have been attempts to put me into **SHIZO** and even straight into **PKT** (and that would be very dangerous). But . . . What would I have done if over these last two years practically half the compound hadn't become my friends? So the authorities held back, cried off – obviously an order had arrived from above telling them not to make a big fuss. But they've certainly taken their toll on my nerves.

Oh to the dogs with them all! Or maybe not! I'd feel sorry for the dogs. They'd eat them whole, tails and all. Taking everything into consideration, to Hell with them! I would express myself more strongly, but, in the first place, you don't approve of women swearing, and in the second place it's a pity somehow to use the language of the camp less than twenty-four hours before being freed. Let's leave them to their own fate.

Are there really only a couple of days to go before . . . ?

No, darling. I won't go to your relatives on the first day. There's mother: I shall spend the first day with my own family. And then the day after (God, it's only the day after tomorrow – God willing, of course!) I shall visit your family first thing in the morning. I hope that there will already be a letter there waiting for me. I will visit your home, go into your room, see first of all 'Night', 'Self-Portrait', 'Woman Who Has Lost Her Child', 'Vision', and then find the letter for me on your desk . . . I shall sit, in convict fashion, on the floor, open the envelope and begin to read the letter, and Cheshka the dog will come over to me, lick my ear and lie down beside me. And I shall read out to her what her master says. I wonder whether Cheshka will recognize me? Or whether she will suddenly detect an unfamiliar scent and bark at me.

No, I am simply not in a condition to write. Forgive me, my darling. And everyone is pestering me to say goodbye to them, and I've still got a hundred and one things to do, like passing on my final 'collections' for prior transmission to freedom – letters, a few poems, etc. and then I need to give away all my possessions so as not to upset anyone, and then memorize all the commissions and requests – there's no way I could take a list out with me. And then, of course, there's the farewell supper – the usual custom!

There just remain a few words for me to add. These two people never did meet again. He, after all, had the remainder of his sentence to serve, and the rest was achieved by life itself. When he was finally released he married the friend of his former lover. The woman married someone else. All that endures of their love is the bundle of letters which you have just finished reading.

And what has happened to the authors of the other letters? Almost all of them have been released, except three who are still serving out their sentence.

I ought to add the following as well. When I was finishing this book in 1986, a new *List of Political Prisoners in the USSR* was about to be published in Munich. It comes out once a year and reflects the state of affairs on 30 October, Political Prisoners' Day. The new list contains 745 names, including those of fifty women. But these are only the ones we have managed to obtain information about from the USSR. The names of the majority of political prisoners are known only to the Soviet authorities. And among them are many women – mothers, lovers, wives. Their letters you will, perhaps, never read . . .

Julia Voznesenskaya
Munich, 7 January 1987